Karl Rahner
Daniel Morrissey

Theology
of Pastoral Action

The pragmatism of Americans is a
commonplace, but perhaps it is not
so well known that the theologians
of Europe, taking this penchant
for practical creativity more seriously than Americans sometimes
do, look to the English-speaking
world and especially to America
herself for viable developments in
contemporary pastoral theology.
The collaboration of Karl Rahner,
the great German theologian, and
Daniel Morrissey, a young American theologian, in *Theology of Pastoral Action* points this hope up
well—as does the fact that theirs is
the first book in a series intended
specifically to stimulate the development of imaginative pastoral
theology in the American and
British Churches.

continued on back flap

THEOLOGY OF PASTORAL ACTION

STUDIES IN PASTORAL THEOLOGY

edited by

Karl Rahner, S. J., and Daniel Morrissey, O. P.

VOLUME I

THEOLOGY
OF PASTORAL ACTION

by
Karl Rahner

HERDER AND HERDER

1968

HERDER AND HERDER NEW YORK

232 Madison Avenue, New York, N. Y. 10016

BURNS & OATES LIMITED

25 Ashley Place, London S. W. 1

This edition of Karl Rahner's
"Grundlegung der Pastoraltheologie als praktische Theologie",
Handbuch der Pastoraltheologie, I, 2, published by
Herder, Freiburg, 1964,
is translated by W. J. O'Hara and is adapted for an
English-speaking audience by Daniel Morrissey, O. P.

Library of Congress Catalog Card No. 67–18253
First published in West Germany © 1968 Herder KG
Printed in West Germany by Herder

Contents

5

Chapter Two
Christians: Action in the Church

General Introduction to the Series

We launch this new series, *Studies in Pastoral Theology,* with
optimism and confidence, but only after taking it under
consideration for several years. We have deliberated this
length of time because neither the pre-Vatican III Church nor
the pacemaking secular society has the time or interest for
just another theological series. We begin *Studies in Pastoral
Theology* convinced that it will meet a very particular and
urgent need which is still unfulfilled. These studies are
projected and proposed for today's English-speaking world
and are directed to the mission of English-speaking Christians. For that reason one of the editors of the series is an
American theologian, and its contributors will be mainly
writers from the English-speaking churches. The *raison
d'être* of this new series is to stimulate original theological
investigation and reflection in the area in which the Anglo-
Saxon mind, especially the American, shows a unique
practical creativity — pastoral theology.

It is puzzling, but undeniable, that while Western Europe
is greatly concerned with being dominated by the United

States and her Anglo-Saxon allies economically, technically and militarily, the reverse is true in the area of theology: the English-speaking churches are theological satellites of Europe. During the past several years an increasing dissatisfaction with this situation has been apparent throughout the English-language world, especially in the United States and Great Britain. Poor translations, ideas obscured by different and difficult thought and language patterns, and unfamiliar historical and philosophical structures have all served to sharpen the awareness of the theological inbalance between Europe and the New World. This is, however, a concern which is shared in Europe where the historic background of Western culture silhouettes the need in the age of space exploration and thermonuclear war for the English-speaking churches to begin to carry their weight theologically. The many facets of life today, the constant changes in city and society, the climbing level of education, the growth of man through communications and technology — all of these factors demand that a vital contribution be made in theology by those countries most influential in forming and developing today's world.

The need for an authentic English-culture theology is widely admitted; it is much more difficult to determine the elements and possibilities of such a theology. For one thing, neither Canada, the United States, nor the Commonwealth is intellectually independent; all are part of Western (which is not simply European) culture. Theologically that community has been recognized and maintained by the impact of translations. Kant, Freud, and Heidegger deeply influence our attitudes toward science, toward conscience and religion, toward time and human existence, and during the past ten years De Lubac, Congar and Küng, and Teilhard de Chardin have been the great names in theology on both sides of the Atlantic. Any theology from the English churches will always share the broader characteristics of the Western mind even as it works out a reflection on God, man and society which is unique in its understanding of the secular city of 1968. A multi-dimensioned study of the newly discovered scriptural and liturgical word, of the Church, language, war and peace, city and citizen, race and sexuality — it is here that the new trend of English-culture theological influence throughout the worldwide Church will come to maturity. *Studies in Pastoral Theology* offers a forum to English-speaking Christians as they begin this work.

There are obvious points of similarity between this new series and the *Quaestiones Disputatae,* which attempt to revive from the great ages of Catholic theology a tradition of discussion and inquiry. The earlier series is more academic, more scholarly and could perhaps take as a patron Thomas Aquinas. For these pastoral studies our patron might well be Augustine, forging out a theology for his Roman-African diocese directly from his experiences with his people. *Studies in Pastoral Theology* will raise immediately practical questions in the hope of inspiring both the reflection and the action necessary in the renewal of Christian life today.

The development of a mature and creative theology by the English churches is more complex and sobering, however, than the encouraging summons to begin independent work. At the heart of all that follows is the understanding of the nature of theology, theology seen as total human reflection on God's special revelation in Jesus Christ to a defined individual or group. Then we ask: What is this human theological reflection for Americans? For Australians? What are its sources, its direction, its future, its mainstream and its various currents? This human reflection on Christ as word and event — pastoral theology — not only speaks about God, it also speaks about man. Pastoral theology can and must have a basic man-centered emphasis without ceasing to be Christo-centric or theocentric. Theology has always been ontological and reflective, but today it must be historical and man-centered as well, speaking about both God and man but in man's language. A creative, active, pastoral theology is essentially social, concerned with man and human relationships, and it is also fundamentally communal, oriented to man living in the sociotechnical secular city. It is precisely here that English pastoral theology can make its unique contribution — an original, practical, concrete, applicable word about God and man *today*. Pastoral theology must be existential: man is capable of experiencing God's complete gift of himself, but this happens only today, here-and-now. No one understands today quite as connaturally as the Christians from the English cultures, and it is today, the constantly changing contemporary situation, which must be subjected to continual sociological and theological analysis. In today's Church psychology and urbanology are as theologically relevant as patrology. By analyzing and interpreting today — man, church, world — pastoral theology develops the principles and imperative decisions needed for Christian action now and in the future.

Studies in Pastoral Theology will be written by and for Christians in Liverpool, Chicago, and Ottawa, New Delhi and Sydney. In developing the kind of theology we have been describing they will be working within a framework suggested by Paul Tillich and very apt for Catholic theology now and in the future. Tillich called his theological method "correlation", and found in it a way to preserve the reflective and in-depth aspects of theology at the same time as theology breaks out of a self-centered or past-centered circle into permanent dialogue with today's world. Correlation describes theology as the correlating of two poles, the revelation of God in Christ and the situation to which the Christian must speak. Tillich saw the function of theology as the statement of the truth of the Christian message and the interpretation of this truth for every new generation. The method of correlation explains Christian faith through existential questions in mutual interdependence, with theological answers. For that reason the analysis of the human situation employs philosophy and sociology, poetry and the film.

Not only Tillich but every important theologian — Origen, Augustine, Aquinas, Luther — has been aware of the culture to which he spoke. Once these creative theological encounters with one culture had ended, however, they did not and do not adapt to new times. They still have a great deal to say to every generation, but no amount of *post-factum* "relating" can make them a viable theology for a different age. The reverse is also true: even the most up-to-

11

date preaching and catechesis, attempts to help and console, counselling and social action can be superficial, sentimental or totally secular — ultimately irrelevant and useless — if not inspired by contact with the word of faith. Religious sociology, anthropology or political science are not the same thing as pastoral theology, which is fundamentally reflection upon God and his revelation, a reflection faithful to the Gospel and faithful to man.

Any aspect of life within the Church, any Christian mission, any communal and social Christian question can find a place for re-evaluation in this series. Pastors, sisters, educators, social workers, all of those whose Christian concern is expressed through action are invited to help in giving this series the relevance and conceptual exactitude needed for valuable theological contribution. *Studies in Pastoral Theology* must be practical, but not too practical: its testing, implementation, and application must be carried out in the immediate context of sociotechnical culture. A theology of the parish, for example, cannot be formulated definitively in these pages. What is the parish? How did it come into our society? Where is it moving? Who forms a parish? What is the role of the priest? What is the relationship between parish and diocese? The experience and experimentation with the "floating parish" in Oklahoma, the parish for entertainers and actors in London, the Puerto Rican parish in New York: those who realize the parish in these concrete circumstances must join with those whose social and theological skills will be made available in our pastoral series, and together we can formulate a creative and dynamic pastoral theology of the parish for tomorrow's

Church. By keeping the size of the individual volumes to reasonable limits, we hope that *Studies in Pastoral Theology* will be useful, not only in an immediately practical manner for a Church in change but also useful in the fundamental light of the New Testament and of the Second Vatican Council.

It should be clear, then, that we are not concerned with arriving at precise conclusions since today's facts and rules may well be inaccurate or irrelevant tomorrow. We hope through these volumes to articulate new problems, to bring to light new possibilities, suggestions, indications of how psychology, city-planning, or economics may illumine our faith in God's Word. Ecumenical dialogue with its emphasis on Scripture, the New Hermeneutic, the God-is-dead movement — these forces which bring us back to the life, the words, the history of Jesus Christ show us how profoundly ecumenical pastoral theology is. Our concern in these volumes will be the revelation and the world shared by all Christians. *Studies in Pastoral Theology* has the same goal as the Upsala convocation of the World Council of Churches: Jesus Christ, Word and event, who says to us: "Behold, I make all things new" (Rev. 21:5).

Karl Rahner, S. J.
Daniel Morrissey, O. P.

Preface

Several years ago a prominent French Dominican whose co-workers include several of our century's most important theologians said to me: "After taking part in the Council I am convinced that the future of the Church lies principally with the New World, just as the Church's past history has been written here in Europe." When I took this up and urged him to do all he could to encourage young European theologians to go to America to study and to gain experience, he frowned and asked, "But why?" The devastating candor of his "why" showed that his statement about the Church of tomorrow was not meant as a compliment but was only a rather sad prediction. The Christian future of which he spoke belonged to the New World by inevitability, not by merit. Even though the action was across the ocean, it did not necessarily follow that anything was to be learned there in terms of theological maturity or of deeper understanding of the thought forms necessary for speaking about God in today's multi-level society.

In the months which have passed since that conversation

a great deal has happened in churches of the New World and in the English-speaking churches around the globe. Amazing forward steps have been taken academically and pastorally in ecumenism and liturgical reform, in social sciences, religious life, personal relations, the structures of parochial life, schools, catechetics, social struggle, and perhaps most important is the increasingly sophisticated understanding of the truly neutral character of a pluralistic society. Nonetheless, to say that here is where the real action is in the Church is not to say that here is where intellectual and theological creativity and growth are to be found. The original "why" is still valid and in fact must be posited. Action is not reflection, and if action is to do any more than be a stopgap for the needs of the moment, if action is to be growth and have lasting effects, forming a superstructure for the future, then ecclesial activity must be the expression and formulation of a correlated pastoral theology.

Theology of Pastoral Action is an attempt to provide the kind of creative theological reflection necessary for relevant and effective pastoral life and activity. The book is an analysis of the nature and personality of the Church based upon its lived experience and designed for the Church of tomorrow. The Church is not simply the reflection of the Christ-event as it happened several millenia ago. Psychologists tell us that a generation now lasts about seven years. If God's self-disclosure in Jesus Christ is to make any sense at all to a constantly changing culture and society, then revelation must undergo a continual historical and critical examination together with the twentieth century to which it is proclaimed. This book, the first of a new series of volumes of pastoral theology, is the result of Karl Rahner's thirty years of theological reflection on the Church from a pastoral perspective.[1] It is only a background study, a kind of white paper designed to be of use to the many different types of pastoral specialists and theologians who work in today's English-language secular city.

Originally we had planned to open the series with a volume entitled *What Is Pastoral Theology?* We realized, however, that this important question cannot be raised except in the context of the Church. Pastoral theology reflects upon the Church's self-realization today and from that draws conclusions about the forms in which it will express itself tomorrow. *Theology of Pastoral Action* as an introductory volume emphasizes our intention to consider every pastoral question from an ecclesial point of view.

Until recently theology looked upon itself as a systematic ordering of a body of intellectual truths with new ideas to be logically deduced from them. In the very nature of things an ordered structure of premises and conclusions could be discovered: the sources of revelation, tradition and Scripture expressed the faith in statements which then served the

[1] Father Rahner is the author of the first volume of this series and he hopes by inaugurating it to stimulate and to attract original and authentically English-church contributions for the following volumes. Some readers will be familiar with the 2000-page *Handbuch für Pastoraltheologie* which Father Rahner edits. This new series is not to be confused with a translation of the German *Handbuch,* nor is it to be thought of as a textbook of pastoral theology in installments. *Studies in Pastoral Theology* is uniquely planned to deal with issues which concern those whose mission is to bring Christ to the English-speaking world.

function of the major premise of a syllogism. Logic and metaphysics enabled new syllogistic conclusions to be drawn from the statements of faith, and these conclusions were theology. This conceptualized and intellectualized belief tended to take theology and faith out of their natural context of concrete human life. That God revealed himself in word and event through history among men as recorded in the narrative of Scripture — this was never denied, but it was neglected for an overly rational accent. Also over-looked were psychological and sociological reflection and their role in proclaiming the Christian message anew to a vital, changing, pluralistic world.

This abstract theology spoke of the Church in terms of mystery. The impression was given that God had not so much revealed himself or his love or even his plan for mankind but rather had shown us the mystery of the Church through the life and death of Christ. God as truth and love is mysterious, as are salvation-history and Jesus Christ, but they are mysteries which in their very nature are related to concrete human life. It is in this way that Karl Rahner reflects upon the Church as it reveals God to men in the latter part of the twentieth century.

When Father Rahner proposed *Studies in Pastoral Theology* and wrote *Theology of Pastoral Action* he showed himself very much aware of the worldwide implications of the English-culture churches' individuality and responsibility. He did not intend in any way, however, to encourage a nationalistic, provincial pattern of Christian thought, nor is the series self-consciously trying to demonstrate that the Americans or Scots or Irish are just as intelligent as the

18

French, Germans, or Dutch. What these volumes do wish to show, in somewhat the same way as Herbert W. Richardson's provocative *Toward An American Theology*,[2] is that Anglo-Saxon thought and culture has its own authentic resources and talent for the development of theology in an affluent society and a nuclear age.

The growing scientific, economic and cultural influence of the United States throughout the world and especially in western Europe stands in ironic contrast to the Americans' theological dependence. Until now the United States has been theologically underdeveloped and has relied heavily upon outside support and aid. The situation is already changing, however, as is demonstrated by the impact in Europe of Harvey Cox's *The Secular City*. The social force of the United States is the explanation for the book's global theological and cultural significance. Cox's reflection on man today and tomorrow in relation to the Gospel coupled with a sure use of contemporary analysis-sociology is particularly American in the best sense: it could not have been done as well or as naturally by a theologian who had not been formed in and by the pace-setting American society.

Nonetheless, even granted the necessity and the possibility of a creative English-language theology there are many complex problems: What about the quantity and quality of Catholics professionally trained in disciplines ranging from psychoanalysis and mass-media to phenome-

[2] Herbert W. Richardson, *Toward An American Theology*, New York: 1967.

19

nology? Would an authentic British or American pastoral theology be simply a matter of method, a new theological approach? Should theological brainpower be joined to the general cultural influences in our society, or is it more a question of theology contributing directly and in depth to man's discovery of himself? How can an American theology retain its Western and European roots even as it develops its own specifically American character? In searching for answers to these questions it must be remembered that a creative English theology must be correlative, a vital encounter between church and theology and the basic structures of society. Today European theology, liturgy and social struggle lack that spontaneous, creative note because they are still primarily devoted to halting the de-Christianization of historically Christian nations. The successful revival of the priest-workers (not the worker-priests) in France is not an exploration into new forms of Christian contact and mission as much as it is an effort to bind up a gaping wound. In contrast the eleventh, twelfth and thirteenth centuries created a pastoral theology which was the natural result of a progressing Church in tune with man and his world. Today it is the English-speaking countries and churches which pioneer and set standards; it is now our Christian opportunity and responsibility to establish the dialogue between pastoral practice and theological reflection.

Theology of Pastoral Action is a pastoral ecclesiology. It is intended to be applied to concrete situations, but the author does not accomplish this final and most important step; he offers only guidelines which must then be tested and applied or rejected by the individual Christian in his own community. We are the Church, the learning and listening Church, which is to say that we are all theologians, actively and creatively helping to formulate the theology for our particular Christian situation. Gone is the day when others can hand us the answers, the manuals, the *summas*. Ours is a do-it-yourself theology. Karl Rahner is far from a Negro parish in Milwaukee, far from a newspaper office in Edinburgh, far from a university campus in Toronto, but the Christians who read these pages are not.

The tentative proposals, the hypotheses in this book, need creative analysis and application. They also need that vital contact with experimentation which is another aspect of pastoral theology. Revelation and reflection must be correlated with the new life-forms and possibilities open to the people who hear the Word now. What Rahner has to say about ecclesial office or diocese or parish is the result of a lifetime of theological and pastoral reflection. But it is far from the last word. *Theology of Pastoral Action* develops questions and problems but only outlines the direction of the answers. This book is actually only the second of four steps involved in an authentic English-language pastoral theology, a re-thinking of the basic Christian kerygma so that it can be communicated to a particular group. First, there is the acceptance and the understanding of the kerygma gained by theology, a vital, active acceptance which includes the study of past reflection on revelation, the theologies and systems of other times. Second, we attempt to correlate Christ to society, revelation to contemporary culture and man, the Good News to our own times. This articulation

21

can be realized through many different dimensions of human reflection, and it is here — in communication — that pastoral theology is seen to be homocentric at the same time that it is theocentric. Of primary concern are the sociological and psychological formation of the hearers, media such as television, publications, liturgy, philosophical frameworks, economic and educational patterns. This book is an example of this second moment in theology. Third, there follows an awareness and consideration of the new and most recent pastoral experience of the Church, the viable, moving Church revealed in experimentation with different forms of life and activity, of sacrament, liturgy, education, religious life, apostolic witness. Reflection and tentative supposition must be tested against creative expression through new forms of activity and life. The fourth and final step is deciding upon a course of action and implementing it. Kerygma, correlation, experimentation combine to produce action for today's and tomorrow's Church.

Whether *Theology of Pastoral Action* is concerned with the nature of the Church or with a national bishops' conference, or perhaps offers a passing observation on celibacy and the diaconate, the book points up relationships which have been neglected before and reveals structural principles which integrate the various missions within the pastorale[3] of the Church today. In the section on the papacy, for

---

[3] *Pastorale* is a word I have taken from the French to express pastoral action or pastoral activity. Each Christian is responsible for a particular pastorale, a particular mission in which he realizes God in his own society. Because the term is so apt for the subject matter of this book it is used frequently; it is not a Rahnerian term, however.

example, only the most basic principles of the pope's pastoral and magisterial offices are outlined. Probably there is no account available of what the Holy See does in all of its various spheres of activity, no methodical and systematic explication of the principles of papal pastoral action. Consequently, if the ideas seem incomplete and the style somewhat abrupt, it is because *Theology of Pastoral Action* is neither a complete nor a proportioned ecclesiology; it offers suggestions for a pastoral ecclesiology which must be realized and developed in the local churches. The first chapter is admittedly more abstract and difficult than the second. But the practical and concrete observations offered in the latter section of the book cannot be understood correctly and will be taken out of context as little more than slogans unless they are seen as the outgrowth of the theology of the Church with which the study begins.

Ultimately action in the Church — the relationships between individuals and groups within the People of God — takes place in the local church. Before Vatican II the local church was seen as only a part of the universal Church. Trent overemphasized the significance of the world Church, and it was for our own council to give a broad vision of the local church and to see in it the actualization and historical revelation of the one Church of Christ. We are the Church, and it is of our church — our particular English-language church — that we should be thinking as we read these pages.

Because of the ingrained tendency to absolutize, almost eternalize many of the elements in the Church, we have forgotten the provisional nature of its theological formulae, the mutability of its norms, the adaptability of its rites. An excellent example of the flexibility and supple reflection *Studies in Pastoral Theology* hopes to stimulate is Herbert McCabe's essay presenting the Church in the new analogy of a culture.[4] McCabe suggests the possibility of comparing the Church to an area of communication, and his ideas are both contemporary and original, capable of varied applications within the Christian pastorale. Another example of authentic, creative pastoral theology is the Association of Chicago Priests' symposium, "Ministry in the Church", in which the role of the priest was discussed in great depth in terms of secularity, experimentation, the urgency of the present situation, and the vision, hope and opportunity of the present and future.[5]

Theology of Pastoral Action is a call for the English-language churches to stand up and be counted theologically. It is a summons to produce a dynamic and creative reflection on God's word of love to man today. This pastoral theology has a long way to go. It has been long in coming, and it is only in its beginnings. But it has come. It has begun. And it will continue as it has begun, by God and man working together in the secular city.

Daniel Morrissey, O.P.

[4] Herbert McCabe, O. P., "The Church and the World", in *The Meaning of the Church,* ed. Donal Flanagan, Dublin: 1966, 55–72.
[5] The symposium, "Ministry in the Church", was sponsored in November, 1967, by the Association of Chicago Priests at the University of Chicago's Center for Continuing Education. Participants included Edward Schillebeeckx, Michael Novak, Andrew Greeley, Bernard Cooke, Thomas F. O'Meara, Bernard Häring and others. The papers and discussions of the symposium are soon to be published.

CHAPTER ONE

The Church: Basis of Pastoral Action

Pastoral theology deals with the action of the Church. It is pastoral because it engages concrete circumstances; it is theological because it reflects systematically on the nature of the Church and analyses the circumstances which confront the Church today. A theology of the Church in action and of action in the Church presupposes, therefore, a knowledge of the Church's abiding nature, and for this one turns to ecclesiology and dogmatic theology. The work of pastoral theology begins only when Christians here and now and at a local level incarnate the Church's nature. Still dogmatic theology's task of portraying the fundamental nature of the Church must be considered by the pastoral theologian at least in a summary way. The reasons are clear. Dogmatic ecclesiology is a relatively young branch of theology: it has not yet attained such dimensions and general acceptance that its findings can be taken for granted. Furthermore, a basic essential ecclesiology is needed in order to establish *a concrete, existential ecclesiology,* for this is what pastoral theology is. Because we are directly concerned with the problems of pastoral theology, our theoretical ecclesiology will have its own individual form and emphasis, that of a summary description of the nature of the Church drawn up for the purposes of pastoral theology.

1. *Fundamental Nature of the Church*

We must specify the *fundamental* nature of the Church because there can be no question of discussing *in extenso* all aspects of her nature. The Church's radical nature might be described in biblical terms as the New Covenant of God's people, the Body of Christ, etc. Since, however, nothing short of a presentation and analysis of all such biblical terms could produce an ecclesiology adapted to our purposes, we shall not employ this method but shall rather attempt to state the fundamental nature of the Church in terms which, although they will always refer to the biblical statements, nevertheless express more directly the unity and multiplicity of the Church's nature.

The Church is the community, legitimately constituted in a social structure,[1] *in which through faith, hope and love God's*

---

[1] We presuppose here the distinction between community and society. We use "community" to denote unity among men resulting from and constituted by that which makes them spiritual and free persons. By "society" we mean the unity among men which is a consequence of their bodily, sexual, spacial, material nature and which seeks to give historical expression to their community. In the Church men's community is manifest by their forming a society (in worship, law, sacraments) in which they are spiritual persons favoured with God's self-communication.

26

eschatologically definitive revelation (his self-communication) in Christ remains present for the world as reality and truth.

There can only be a Church in the eschatological stage of divine revelation because it is only then that the dialogue relation between God and creature — God's absolute self-communication to man (Incarnation and grace) — is absolutely and irrevocably present. It is only eschatologically that God's historical self-communication comes to be known explicitly for what it is, known in the historical Christ-event and in the Church's confession of faith in Christ. Mankind *is* the Church to the extent that man really accepts this absolute self-communication of God, eschatologically irrevocable in Christ and his grace. Man's acceptance is brought about by God's self-communication and is the way the divine self-giving becomes historically present — in the proclaimed word of faith, in the ritual enactment of the eschatological saving event, and in the unity of a society.

The Church is, therefore, both the gift of salvation and the means of salvation. The Church is the *gift* of salvation — the term and realization of God's self-communication — because it is the historical, socially organized community of those who accept and confess God's self-communication in Christ and his Spirit, divinizing men and forgiving sinners. The Church is also a *means* of salvation because in the solemn confession of this community God utters the operative, efficacious word in which he wills to give himself and does effectively give himself to the world and to each individual.[2]

[2] From the ultimate identity of the Church as gift of salvation and as means of salvation it follows — and this is a fundamental insight in

THE CHURCH: BASIS OF PASTORAL ACTION

This conception of the Church involves certain assumptions. God's redemption concerns and claims every dimension of man, including the historical and social. Salvation itself is historical, i.e., without detriment to the possibility of salvation for every individual human being in every age, this self-communication of God to mankind is an historical process. In the first place, it is only in Christ that it is found irrevocably, victoriously and definitively established. Second, in this self-communication God is not only outside history as its transcendent ground but himself enters temporally and spatially into history. Third, the history of the empirical, social and conscious realization of this self-communication of God to all men, perpetually taking place throughout all history, is yet another factor in God's self-communication: in this way it imparts its own temporal character to created history. For the conscious explication and objectification in the Church of word, worship and confession of faith are made possible and supported by grace, in other words by God's self-giving.

Revelation is essentially a revelation-event, a deed of God, because it does not consist merely in human discourse but conveys the very reality of what is revealed. A revelation heard and accepted occurs as faith. Now if faith is not to reduce God's word to merely human discourse about God

---

pastoral theology — that ultimately the Church is apostolically active by being given ever anew as a gift of salvation, always allowing itself to be built up anew by God in faith, hope and love. Conversely, the Church allows itself to be renewed by God in this way by apostolically bearing witness for the world, not thinking of itself and its own self-affirmation.

(because of the created *a priori* conditions of the human mind's hearing), it can exist only when based on God's grace. This means that what is heard and believed is not only the object, but also the subjective principle of faith. The history of salvation, of grace, of divine self-communication and of revelation has a strict identity and constitutes one and the same history both in the transcendental, supernatural condition of its *possibility* (grace as a supernatural, existential and subjective cognitional horizon of any possible word-revelation) as well as in its *actual historical form* (revealed word of God, Incarnation, Church). This history of God's self-communication reaches its eschatological culmination in Christ: there it has become irrevocable within history itself and in this sense is historical. It has attained perfect empirical, historical objectivation in word and in human society, and yet remains present. All the subsequent history of man's knowledge and freedom now takes place under this objectified, transcendental dimension of Christ's redemptive history, a history constituted gratuitously through God's self-communication. This is what we call the Church in contradistinction to the Synagogue and other socially organized phases of the pre-Christian history of salvation and revelation (and in contradistinction, therefore, to other earlier world religions).

2. The Church as Presence of God's Truth and Love

The Church is the historical and social presence of God's self-communication to the world in Christ. God reveals and

29

communicates himself ("uncreated grace"), as *sign of salvation,* the manifest word of God (speaking, spoken and heard). This presupposes that the Church both *is* and *acts*. This unity of potency and act is the distinguishing mark of personal, free, spiritual beings. In them an action reverts to the essence in which it is grounded, determines this, and by manifesting it, brings it to identity with itself, so that act and potency have their unity in diversity. The Church has this kind of unity of what it is ("society") and in what it does (proclamation of the word, confession of faith, worship, life). This is the Church: the eschatologically perfect self-giving of God to humanity in the historical and social domain.

For pastoral theology the whole problem is to determine precisely and comprehensively exactly what should become "present" in today's Church in this way. The Church is not simply an institution which follows divine instruction to seek the salvation of the individual man or woman. It is more than a useful society with divine help and a significant opinion about God and salvation. Above and beyond all else the Church is the concrete embodiment of God's salvation, the presence of God (not God himself present, which would be heresy and yet remains the permanent temptation of the Church). If we are to say what the Church really has to do and in what activities it realizes its own nature, we must know precisely what becomes present in the Church, what gives itself to men in the Church, constituting the Church as a saving presence, uniting God and man. A pastoral theologian cannot of course sharply separate the question of how the Church at any given moment is to carry out its own specific function from the consideration of what those functions are. The first question nevertheless remains: What does become really present in the Church? Only in this way can we hope to deal with the question of the Church's pastoral action in today's world.

1. God gives himself to man. This self-giving takes place in history, in faith and hope, and not in that immediacy of eternal life where we will possess the gift in its plenitude. It occurred definitively in Jesus Christ and irrevocably established its acceptance; it has an enduring, historical, empirical, social presence and manifestation. This is the Church — the enduring expression of Christ accepted as God's definitive gift and promise of himself to mankind. Consequently, the authentic activity of the Church is found when man is made open to God, God as he is in himself and for us. Man can be opened to the absolute, nameless mystery who, uncircumscribed, immeasurable, in his own indefinability is both ground and unfathomable abyss, measure and measureless in one. God as God becomes present in the Church; he is the living God, the destruction of every claim to finality on the part of anything specified or controlled, the end of all polytheistic idolatry.

The Church, therefore, precisely by what it is, is an institution in conflict with anything purely institutional which claims to take the place of God. If revolution means the denial of what represents itself as definitive, then the Church is a permanent revolution. For ultimately its sole purpose is to give honor to God and to save man by perpetually compelling him to relinquish anything which he takes to be definitive, and to capitulate before the God who is possessed as true God only if really, and not merely in words, he is confessed to transcend everything outside him, everything we can conceive. God makes our own transcendent orientation towards him a mystery to ourselves, beyond our control. The Church continues to be a permanent revolution, destroying idols; it has not mistaken the whole business of religion for God himself (the essential temptation), and therein lies the abiding marvel of the grace promised to the Church.

The Church always discovers this grace with astonishment, turning it to self-criticism in serene awareness that such criticism of its own actual performance is an element in its nature, inherent in it and requiring no horizon beyond that of the Church itself. The infinite horizon of all human criticism, God himself, gives himself to the Church in grace, with self-criticism as a form of that grace. The Church confesses the God-man as the presence of God; because it understands man as the destroyer of all idols in virtue of his liberation by grace. The Church adores in faith when it transcends the conditions its own existence implies. It adores in hope when it transcends the present into the unknown future of God the incomprehensible. It adores in love when it trusts and fervently accepts God's radical incomprehensibility as the gift of his love. The Church knows him whom it adores only in this liturgy of adoration, because only in this way is the inexpressible present.

2. This presence of God in the Church constituted by his absolute, eschatological self-communication is, nevertheless, not inexpressible simply because in it presence and absence, acceptance or refusal amount to the same thing.

32

God's presence has to be experienced and accepted in its transcendental immediacy and irreductibility. Man, nevertheless, must consciously reflect on and conceptually objectify this presence of mystery as the ground of his being. This presence, without ceasing to be that of the abiding, ineffable mystery, has so true a dual character of the presence of God himself that the duality of his presence in the Church is an aspect of God in and for himself.

God is present in the Church as truth and as love. God's self-communication, which gives God as he is in himself, comes in this double mode of presence as a mode of being of God in himself. God remaining uncircumscribed in this presence (as the "Father") gives himself as absolute love (in the Spirit). This double mode of his action towards us is also the mode of his own being.[3] This is not the place to discuss the mystery of the two "processions" and the dogmatic theology of the Trinity. What is in question here is the clear development of the fundamental fact that Christian salvation is not just any kind of action of God in regard to man. It is God's self-giving which is so truly that of God himself that its radical nature cannot be thought of as other than it is, other than expressing this very duality of the inner-Trinitarian processions. The Trinity of the economy of redemption is the immanent Trinity. *The duality of the inner-Trinitarian processions forms the basis of the presence of God in the Church and is therefore the basis of the nature of*

---

[3] This is in no way a metaphysical deduction of the mystery of the Trinity because the "deduction" starts from the "economical Trinity" which can only be experienced in a non-reflex manner in grace and can only be known explicitly from (official) revelation.

the Church. If the nature of the Church is to be elucidated, nothing more "intelligible" or simpler will suffice.

The Church is primarily the presence of God. The Father reveals himself and gives himself to be possessed as the truth uttered in the Son, and in so doing remains Father, incomprehensible mystery, mystery uttered in the Word. The Church is the presence of God first and foremost as truth, the truth in which God communicates himself. The Church is both the eschatological gift of salvation and the means of salvation; it accepts the Word of God in faith and confesses and bears witness to God's truth. That the Church is the Church of the truth heard with belief and proclaimed, a truth which is absolute mystery present to it, is essentially the first characteristic of the Church and therefore of its pastoral action. It must be noted that when God gives himself as truth, he is already salvation (light, life). His truth must not be misconceived as a collective sum of human propositions; it is God's gracious self-giving in his actual, real Word, who by his own reality is the basis of man's conceptual knowledge of revelation.

The Church is primarily a gift of salvation and only consequently a means of salvation. Even the apostles had to believe first in order to be capable of becoming bearers of revelation. The only preacher who did not have to hear and believe first was Christ. The Church's activity as the presence of truth must therefore always have such a form that it is evident and visible to the world that the teaching Church in the accomplishment of its mission to the world listens, hears, and believes. It must be clear that the Church believes during this age before the fulfillment — during the time when faith is an ever new grace, subject to temptation, when its conceptual and intellectual element is always a means subordinated to prayerful contemplation, when without words and in a way beyond complete analysis a revelation is experienced which consists in God's self-communication in the grace of faith.

The claim of the magisterium is always an appeal to an authority present in the Church of faith; it is an active functioning of the hearing faith of the Church as a whole in contradistinction to the multitude of individuals as such. The faith of the whole Church instructs the individuals because in its faith is the presence of the truth of God. This teaching authority is indefectible because it is the act of those in whose testimony the faith of the Church as a whole receives a truly historically tangible presence of total commitment in faith. The magisterium can speak in the name of the whole Church[4] because the hearing faith of the Church as a whole is indefectible. The Church fulfills its nature as the presence of God's truth when it believes, lives an act of faith, remembers its faith, accepts with praise what is bestowed as God's truth. It says to God what he has said to the Church, gives thanks and celebrates the anamnesis of "tradition" in which the truth is given really (although before conceptual reflection): This alone is the

[4] This speech of the representatives of the Church testifying in their unity to what they have heard in faith is, of course, addressed both to the individual in the Church, who in this way receives the possibility of believing with the Church in which God's truth is really present as grace, as well as to the "world", the unbelievers, to whom the mission is directed.

source of the act in which the Church authoritatively teaches its own members and preaches to non-Christians. But it is clear that even here the Church's activity is not identical with the acts of the official ministry. All believers in the Church together constitute the one free acceptance, empowered by God's self-revelation, of the Father's self-utterance in the Word which was made flesh; they constitute the Church by giving the first inner-Trinitarian procession a presence in the economy of redemption, in the realm of the non-divine and its history.

How does this theology of the first believing action of the Church stand in relation to the traditional classification of the Church's powers into power of order *(potestas ordinis)* and power of jurisdiction *(potestas jurisdictionis)*, or into the three offices of teacher, priest, and pastor? Naturally, we are concerned with the fundamental distinction in the activity of the Church as a whole (the question of what the Church is and does as the presence of God's self-communication), whereas these classical distinctions are those of the Church's ministry or of the offices of the ministry. If, however, the traditional distinctions are really standard ones, they must reflect the nature of the Church as a whole even if basically they concern the Church's ministry alone.[5]

---

[5] It can be assumed that the three "offices" are to be derived from the two powers. The question is: What is the relationship between the believing Church and the power of order and the power of jurisdiction?

The meaning of these two standard powers and the distinction between them is more subtle than is often realized. Their differentiation is not based upon theoretical considerations. An ordination, even if assumed to be valid, confers certain sacred powers which cannot

When we seek an adequate theological basis for drawing a material distinction within the one total activity of the Church and consequently in the ultimately one ministry of the Church, the traditional distinction between power of order and power of jurisdiction does not rule out our basic statement regarding God's self-communicating presence to his Church as truth and love. The latter is more fundamental than the former, which refers to a gradation in the order of the sacred whereby the exercise and transmission

be taken away from the validly ordained person (because they never are). Ordination also confers other powers so that they cannot be exercised all the time and in every case. The one set of powers is called powers of order *(potestates ordinis)*, and the other powers of jurisdiction *(potestates jurisdictionis)*.

This description of powers of order does not prove the popular assumption that the Church cannot "bind" the exercise of certain powers in such a way that their use is not merely illicit but actually invalid. Granted that baptism by heretics and pagans (Denz. 860) can be valid, it is open to debate whether this principle can be applied to other cases of the exercise of a power of order. It is certainly possible that powers of order can be bound so that actions performed in contradiction to their prohibition are not only illicit but invalid. (Denz. 196, 424, 584, 854, etc., refer mostly to particular cases — sins which cannot be absolved by just any power of order — or simply state a fact without declaring that it is impossible *in principle* for the Church to "bind" the powers of order).

It cannot be assumed from the description of powers of jurisdiction that ordination has nothing directly to do with them. Were that the case, then absolute ordination would become the norm. This would clearly contradict the history of the Church and Canon Law and the dogmatic instinct of Christendom, which has always regarded relative ordination as the norm of holy orders.

The distinction between powers of order and jurisdiction so familiar in the practical life of the Church is often thought to be based on intrinsic differences in their natures. The power of order would comof sacred "power" is a sacramental or non-sacramental act according to the degree to which the Church is involved in it.

The Church's action involves the presence of God's truth and love and means a communication of the inner-Trinitarian processions. We are not raising the question here as to which concrete acts of the Church (in teaching, administration of the sacraments, law-making, etc.) refer to one or other of these fundamental functions. We have

prise powers of administering the sacraments *ex opere operato,* and the power of jurisdiction would be made up of powers of direction and rule. The powers of authority would be contradistinguished against the powers of conferring and sustaining life. Theologians who argue, however, that the power of order involves an interior, ontological endowment as compared with the external, pastoral power of juris-diction presuppose an arbitrary and inconclusive theology of sacra-mental character and causality.

Furthermore, the power of administering the sacrament can imply the authority to alter the status of the recipient so that his legal position in the Church is changed. In such a case the power of order is itself one of jurisdiction or implies it. Obviously it cannot be impossible in principle for the conferring of legal powers to take place in and through a sacramental act (e.g., the legal contract of marriage between Christians). Consequently what are usually called power of order and power of jurisdiction are not distinguished as a power which is purely that of dispensing grace in contrast to a power of juridical authority. Both concern the juridical power which is irrevocably given by holy orders itself and the juridical authority which can either be conferred without a sacrament or in a "bound" manner by the sacramental act of ordination. In the second case of a "merely" jurisdictional authority, the Church's authorization is then required for the valid exercise of a power in itself conferred by the sacrament but in a restricted manner. Fundamentally, however, this is only the necessary authorization for the validity of the exercise of a sacramentally conferred power; it does not even decided whether these two fundamental functions of the Church can take concrete form in different acts, each of which would be an exclusive realization in the Church of truth or of love. Nor is it yet clear when the activity of the Church as the presence of truth has an official character, actually involves a divine right, constituting the "magisterium". The activity of the Church even in this domain cannot be equated with the activity of the Church's ministry, e.g., its teaching capacity.

not confer the power which is to be exercised, for this is conferred sacramentally. In some cases, the necessary authorization for the valid exercise of a sacramentally conferred power (for example the assignment of a particular territory to a consecrated bishop, or the granting of faculties for hearing confessions) is simply an aspect of the nature of the case which belongs intrinsically to the concrete form of a sacramental act of ordination. The power which is conferred by the sacrament involves a plurality of social factors and aspects which need not necessarily be constituted by one action *in indivisibili* at one and the same time. Moreover, there can be acts of jurisdiction which do not engage the ultimate nature of the Church so that the transfer of the Church's authority in regard to them does not deeply commit the Church and for this reason has not the character of a sacramental action. It therefore follows that the distinction between power of order of jurisdiction as it is usually applied (and from the practical point of view rightly so) does not constitute an ultimate objection but really signifies grades of intensity of one and the same power (which of course from other points of view must be distinguished), so that differences in its transmission refer to these.

One real difficulty can be raised against this concept — the papal primacy and its transmission. Because the papal authority is the highest and most comprehensive in the Church, it must be regarded as involving both the sacramental and the juridical orders. The authority of the pope would necessarily be conferred as the highest stage of the sacrament of orders. In answer we can say that it is remarkable that the

3. The second element of God's presence determining the fundamental activity of the Church as a whole is the love of God. It corresponds to the second divine procession and in fact is identical with it. The Church is the presence of God inasmuch as in it the Father reveals himself and gives himself to be possessed as a love which communicates itself in the Spirit. As such it remains an uncircumscribable, but accepted, mystery. Since the Church is both the eschatological gift of salvation as well as the means to salvation, the Church first receives God's love and then gives it to men in sacrament, prayer and life; both receiving and giving belong indefectibly to the Church's nature and

power of order by divine right is said to be three-tiered (bishop, priest, deacon) while the power of jurisdiction is only two-tiered as far as the divine right is concerned (pope, bishops); it is also remarkable that these two hierarchies cannot be mutually co-ordinated. Is the silence of tradition and theological opinion a peremptory argument that the primacy is not a particular and highest degree of holy orders? The way in which it is transmitted does not exclude a positive answer, for it is impossible to show that imposition of hands is necessary and that the tangible mode of induction into the office of pope is insufficient to constitute a sacramental sign.

It has been argued that the acquisition of the primacy should not be called a sacrament because it cannot be "conferred" since there is no higher possessor of this authority to confer it. On this assumption, however, there would no longer be any proof that the primacy is concerned only with the power of jurisdiction. The pope must certainly have himself consecrated bishop if he is to be the highest subject of all authority in the Church in every respect: his jurisdictional authority concerns in the strongest possible way the power of order of the other ecclesial office-bearers. The special case of papal primacy does not destroy the validity of our view of order and jurisdiction as grades of intensity of one power. Cf. also Karl Rahner, *Bishops, Their Status and Function* (New York 1965).

activity, and the two in conjunction make the Church holy.

The Church is the presence of God's eschatologically victorious grace (love) not only in objective holiness (the efficacy of the Church's means of sanctification) but also in subjective holiness, by which the Church can never entirely fall from the grace of God. The bringing to accomplishment of this presence is the act of all those living in God's grace in the Church. In some form they make this love present and perceptible in the Church's historical and social embodiment. To accomplish that presence God's love speaks in the word of the ministry to liberate men's freedom to love, confessing divine love in the actual sacramental word. The accomplishment of that presence also involves active love for God and our neighbours by all Christians in whose life God's love becomes present (and *convincing*) in the world. This presence of God's love is found (as far as ministry is concerned) in the power of order, in the administration of the sacraments. A sacrament is the efficacious word of the Church's (and so of God's) self-donation to the individual. There the Church engages itself absolutely. The Church's word never loses its character or intention of conferring God's love, even when in certain individual cases it does not possess the character of absolute commitment and so cannot be termed a sacrament in the strict sense.

But now we have a new question to consider: Are the two factors by which the Church is the presence of God's self-communication to the world in Christ simply two aspects of one and the same actualization of the Church?

41

Or are they materially different acts of the Church's self-realization in which God's truth acts independently of God's love? Christ has come to give men truth and love. His truth is love, but are they the same?

The actions of the Church can be acts of the presence of truth or of love. An act of the Church's teaching office, for example, is an act of one of the charisms in the Church,[6] and does not demand the presence or power of the entire Church. But the function of the Church as presence of divine truth has as its purpose the presence of love. And where love is genuinely practised, truth as such is also present.[7] Indeed the Church, because it is holy, can never grasp or bear witness to God's truth in such a way as to set itself in absolute opposition to that love of which the Church with eschatological necessity is the presence. Of course the Church must perpetually overcome any contradiction in its life between the presence of truth and of love: Christ's truth should appear as the innermost light of love.

For God truth and love are one, but man, member of community and society, is subject to time and change. Man's temporal character injects concrete, historical contingency into the Church and its life. Today *only history and*

[6] For pastoral practice it is of the greatest importance to acknowledge that each person and each office cannot do everything but only what belongs to it, and that the Church is the unity of what remains diverse, within the love which makes room for all and bears what is different and not understood.

[7] Truth and love have not precisely the same mode of presence here. That is shown in the justification of the individual; he can believe without having charity, but the converse is not possible.

society can tell us about man and his pastoral situation, and only the existing, temporal Church can attain the abiding, necessary, and divine. The distinct actions which fill the Church's life and in which God's truth and love become present can possess different degrees of intensity in different eras and societies. We might consider, for instance, the act of martyrdom, the celebration of the Eucharist, a simple congregational prayer for unity, a practical expression of Christian spirit in social action, etc. — these are all activities of the Church. The official character of each is different, as is the particular grace-given commitment, or the relation between their personal Christian sign and the Christ signified in them, but all incarnate God's love for the world.

3. Characteristics of the Church

Pastoral theology seeks to express correctly in existential theological propositions not only the eschatological parousia in the Church but also God's self-giving presence as truth and love. This is all the more necessary since the eschatological parousia of God in Christ, which we call the Church, has to be distinguished from that self-giving of God in eternity in which he communicates himself face to face to his divinized creature.

1. Mystery

God is present in the Church as mystery. God's approach does not dissolve the mystery which God is, but makes the mystery even more inescapably and sharply apparent.

43

As the Church realizes itself and becomes more and more what it should be, God, Christ and Church become more mysterious.[8] The Church cannot preach its dogmatic teaching or its moral imperatives as a diminution of or defence against God's mystery. Faith and preaching are an ever more ineluctable confrontation with his mystery, a command to enter into believing and loving communication, a grace-given personal meeting with and transcendence of the formula, sign or institution. Ultimately the Church is not the representative of God's honor and gift of salvation for the affairs of our world. God himself becomes present for us as mystery. He does not send a representative in order to avoid personal involvement. The *representation* simply serves to draw our attention to his own *presence*. To draw attention in this way is God's action, which he has the Church perform. The Church is the action of man insofar as God creatively makes possible and actualizes free human action.

2. Primal Sacrament

If we seek a contemporary term to characterize the presence of God's self-communication to the Church and through the Church, and to distinguish this from God's presence

---

[8] This is not the place to develop the importance of this insight for the history of the Church and of human thought in modern times. Atheism is largely only the negative form of a history which Christianity (even as Church) ought positively to have accomplished (with courage to face the growing incomprehensibility of God) but still largely refuses to accomplish.

in final fulfillment, "sacrament" immediately suggests itself. God is so present in the Church that the Church can be called the sacrament of God's self-communication; or to distinguish what we mean from the seven sacraments, we can say that the Church is the most important, the primal sacrament. Naturally Christ is the primordial sacrament, God's fundamental, original sign. As the God-man he is the primordial sacrament because he is what is signified (God in his self-communication to men); he is the efficacious, manifest sign of this self-communication and its acceptance by mankind, for he is man and lives as man in time. The Church is not Christ's abiding presence in the world until his return in such a way that all statements made about Christ as the primordial sacrament of salvation can apply in exactly the same way to the Church. The Church is not identical with Christ: it is not our goal and fulfillment in the same sense as he is. The body of Christ is distinct from him, receives from him, and serves him. Nevertheless, the Church can be called the primal sacrament because, if it were not, there could be no sacraments worthy of the name. The Church's own nature is ontologically prior to the seven sacraments; they are partial realizations of the Church itself. The Church does not simply administer the sacraments; it lives in them, finding its own fulfillment in giving the life of Christ to others.

The expression "primal sacrament" as applied to the Church in many respects expresses the special mode of God's presence in the Church. The Church in its empirical, tangible reality is never identical with its most fundamental concern — God. The Church is only a sign of God. It can never affirm that what is signified (God's grace), is present only where the sign is, i.e., in the Church's historical reality as doctrine, sacrament and society. There is a grace of justification for the "non-Christian". And yet the Church is *the* sign (the primal sacrament) of this grace for the whole world, the sign in which God gives himself not simply to the Church and to those in the Church, but to the world and to all men. Also, all salvation seeks its concrete manifestation in the Church. In this double sense there is no salvation outside the Church. The non-identity between sign and what it signifies relates to the Church as a whole, not only to the sacramental domain in the narrower sense but also to divine truth and its human expression, to moral norm and the practice of the love of God through it, to religious law and personal existential obligation coming directly from God himself. In everything it is and does the Church is a sign which functions by pointing away from itself to God, to God alone, to God as mystery. God must never be confused with his Church. Institutionalism, legalism, clericalism, theological rationalism, objectivist sacramentalism will continually crop up somewhere in the Church, when sign and signified are confused or identified in practice (if not in theory) in any dimension of the Church's life.

The Church is the efficacious manifest sign of the presence of God, its real symbol, containing what it signifies; by grasping the sign man experiences what it signifies. Man finds God's presence in faith and hope, and this search is an historically unfolding movement of men and the Church (as their community) towards their goal, God. This movement has its counterpart in God himself, for he is both the goal and principle (which we call grace) of the movement toward him. The dialectic of the divine presence as goal and as inner principle characterizes God's self-giving in the Church. The Church is the manifest primal sign that God wills to communicate himself to the world, and he brings about the acceptance of his gift with eschatological certainty.

In the Church God is present. Anyone who culpably refuses the historical, empirical form in which God gives himself and insists instead on having God in a purely spiritual way, without his presence in this world, fails to reach God himself. The question of whether there is an empirical, "sacramental" embodiment of God's self-communication and of human movement toward God, an embodiment which is non-ecclesiastical and yet necessary for salvation — this problem essentially depends on a solution (ultimately a merely terminological one) of the question of the factors which constitute the Church. If only those elements are taken into consideration which in the actual circumstances of history distinguish the Roman Catholic Church from others, it would have to be said that there is of course no human being whose transcendental relation to God is not mediated historically, and that this mediation (as freely accepted) is necessary for salvation. We would have to add, however, that such mediation (as really operative and not merely *in voto*) is not necessarily ecclesiastical. If, however (and this is objectively and terminologically more correct),[9] the bond of mankind and other factors of

9 Terminologically more correct because there are of course means of salvation (sacraments, scripture, truth) which certainly cannot be

human reality are counted among those which go to make up the Church, then it can also be said that the Church fundamentally exercises a sacramental function absolutely necessary for salvation even when a man does not belong to it in a sociologically perceptible way.

What is the significance for pastoral theology of these ecclesiological considerations? It is apparent that the Church is the concrete, tangible form and historical embodiment of the promise God addressed to all mankind. Its saving, missionary significance is not solely dependent on the number of its members. The Church's missionary zeal must be based on its awareness that it conveys salvation to the world (as its necessary sign) even where men lay hold of salvation without having wholly understood this sign. The Church is also seeking itself in its missionary activity, not only giving but receiving too when it is successful. For only if the elements of the sign of salvation which are present in all mankind were complete in the Church's historical, empirical form (a goal which in this world is only imperfectly attainable),[10] would the Church be wholly what it is: the primal sacrament which announces salvation

excluded from the realities which go to constitute the Church, even if they are not distinctive solely of the Church. Consequently it is meaning-less terminologically to refuse an ecclesial character to other objective constituts of salvation simply because they can exist even outside full membership of the Church, and indeed even before baptism.

[10] This goal is imperfectly attainable because the Church will always live in conflict until the end of history, as dogmatic eschatology shows. Yet it can never say that among its opponents there are human beings who will be lost. Historically speaking, therefore, the Church always finds itself opposed by some men who are not really its enemies at all,

in such a way that there is no longer reference to any saving element outside itself.

3. New Law of the Gospel

The nature of Church is misunderstood[11] if it is seen as the promulgator of law or as the educator of the human race (and this happens in some measure only too often). When it is thought of as charged with announcing the two ways of truth and love, or as the channel of grace, or as a possibility of salvation placed wholly and entirely under the free decision of the individual human being's acceptance or refusal, the Church's nature is again misrepresented. For the Church is the historical presence in the world of the victorious grace of God, which of itself effects and brings victory with it. That grace confers the possibility of using it and so makes the duty to use it more pressing. Of itself it sets freedom free and gives us our very acceptance of the possibility of salvation, actual salvation itself.

The Church is the presence of the victorious grace of God in which God reveals himself for the salvation of the world, although he could leave it to its ruin: the Church is gospel and not law. Gospel announces the good news and promises

i.e., in their genuine ultimate conception of existence. This situation of still having to seek what really (i.e., through justifying grace) is already its own will never cease while history lasts.

[11] As analysis of the ways Christians misunderstand the Church — clerical triumphalists and lay defeatists — and an appraisal of the Church's limitations and mission in today's society can be found in Karl Rahner, "Should the Church Solve the World's Problems?" *Listening* (Winter, 1967), 4–17.

salvation; law makes demands and promises only that they can be fulfilled. The Church does not proclaim that God *wills* to save the world and to communicate his own glory to it, but that God *has* saved the world and has already given himself to it irrevocably, unconquerably. The Church summons each individual to a life of active combat by proclaiming that God's victory is winning the world. The Church's activity in word, sacrament and life must see itself today as gospel and not simply as law; it must make this intelligible to men in its paradoxical optimism of hope against all hope. Only then can God's parousia in the Church as truth and love have that character of "law" which Christ's parousia has in the New Covenant.

The radical act of God's love in which he gives himself absolutely makes a much more profound demand on man than any created structure of the world (natural law, etc.). But this demand has never come to man from outside, as something exterior, leaving it to him whether to accept or not. It is always a summons (gradually disclosing itself) from God's absolute love, emerging in the innermost (grace-given) center of human reality and bestowing the very thing it demands. God's love for man is the innermost and most real principle of man's love for God. It demands only what it gives, and in this radical demand[12] manifests the innermost glory of God's gift of love. It is the difference

[12] The demand is radical because the "nature" which provides the basis of the law of the new covenant (as a kind of "natural" law) is not a created definable nature (a definite law is followed) but the infinite "nature" of God in which we are given to share and which is itself the law according to which we move.

between the assurance of salvation of the Church as a whole and the uncertainty of individual salvation which gives rise to the character of the gospel as a law which has to be fulfilled. The individual's life unfolds in time and has not yet reached its fulfillment; he is a sinner.

If he has not yet by love and trust in the gospel totally moved away from himself into the Church in which the demands of the law are the radical character of God's powerful, saving and divinizing love for man, then man in his pilgrim, personal life will often experience the law as harsh, external, formal and demanding. Glorying in the grace of God, the Christian *supersedes* the law because God's life is the center of his own personal life: demand and accomplishment are no longer two separate things. Because the Church is the presence of the already eschatologically victorious love of God, it must find its realization as gospel. Only then can it be that law which is freedom and life. If the Church did not perpetually have courage beyond the "facts" of its experience, it would be the Synagogue of the Law, not the Church of the gospel. What applies to the law generally, applies also to the law of the Church for its own members. Like every rule of law it is a summons intelligible only in grace to allow God to give what he demands of us, to accept as his gift what is presented as incumbent on us.

4. *Eschatological Presence*

The Church is an eschatological reality. One day it will cease to exist as a sign, but God will never become "all in all" in such a way that the Church in which he is all will cease to be. The complete accomplishment of his self-communication is man's perfection and fulfillment. Decisive mediating factors such as Christ's humanity, the union of love, personal community and created grace — all constituents of the Church — will continue to have a mediating function in the beatific fulfillment; the Church as sign, however, as social institution, as sacrament of fulfillment belongs to present history and will cease when fulfillment has come.

Beyond this, when we say that the Church is the eschatological presence of God's self-giving, we mean that the history of redemption *is* unfolding and has reached a stage in which it has been irreversibly directed towards the beatifying fulfillment of the world in God by the incarnation and resurrection of the Logos. The explicit counterpart of the history of salvation, its presence in confessing faith, is the Church.

The eschatological character of the Church includes, however, a further element. The explicit, historical expression of God's eschatologically irreversible victory, found in the Church's teaching and profession of faith and in its whole activity in worship and life, has an enduring historical continuity in time. Not only will there always be "Church" in the world, i.e., a social, historical expression of God's self-communication, but there will always be this Church. In spite of the metamorphosis which the Church undergoes in the course of time, it continues to abide in history because of the validity of what it signifies and also because of the verifiability of its historical continuity. The Church as an eschatological reality is not an ever new sign abolish-

52

ing the old; it is the sign and primal sacrament given once and for all, one in history with all its profound changes. Profession of faith in Christ, the word of forgiveness, forms of worship, the constitution of the Church — these do not spring up all of a sudden from a newly discovered ground of reality and transcend history. They demonstrate legitimacy in their unbroken origin from that point in history — Jesus Christ — at which their sacramental character was present for the first time but once and for all. Scripture, apostolic succession, Christ's seven permanent sacraments, the immutable permanence of the fundamental structures of the Church in the Petrine office and in the collegiality of the bishops — all point to the permanence of one Church until the end of time. The Church is not the synagogue with its tangible historical reality under the threat or promise of being superseded.[13]

The eschatological permanency of what in itself is historically *contingent* is of fundamental importance from the point of view of pastoral theology. Under the pressure of the troubles and revolutions of its own age, pastoral theology will always be tempted to derive a new Christianity from society or from abstract theories and to plan it afresh so that it may be really "contemporary". The Church, however, precisely because it is *eschatologically permanent,* is always "traditional". It can change what has been handed down only according to the intrinsic law of Christ's gift.

[13] The Church is not threatened with legitimate replacement by another institution, but does stand under the threat of the second coming of Christ and of the judgment, which even the Church as the actual concrete multitude of human beings will have to face.

To legitimize the new, it appeals to the inner force of the old. It is never revolutionary, because in it all possible human revolutions are already outdistanced by God's most radical revolution. Yet, tradition in its historically contingent form has no special value in itself; tradition is only an attestation to divine revolution. All tradition simply bears witness that Jesus Christ is already risen, that therefore the end of history has already begun, surpassing all religious revolutions.

5. Ever New Actual Presence

The Church as sign of God's eschatological and victorious self-communication in truth and love exists and lives in history. The history of this primal sacramental sign of the world's salvation is the *history* of the final covenant. It is really history.[14] History does not only occur around the Church and on account of it — for instance, the history of the passage of succeeding generations through the Church, or the theological history of the human understanding of the Scriptures, or the concord or conflict of human institutions with the Church, or merely the history of the application of doctrines and principles. Precisely as recipient of salvation (and not merely parallel to this), man is temporal and has a history. The reception of salvation is an important

---

[14] It can be asked whether in the writing of Church history, or prior to it, we have yet elaborated a theology of Church history which understands that Church history is the history of the Church itself, i.e., that the history which ecclesiastical historians relate concerns the Church as a divine institution, and that it ought therefore to be related as such.

element in salvation, for grace produces this reception as it affects man. Redemptive history must continue in the New Covenant; man pursues salvation within his own history.

When we say that the history of revelation closed with the age of the apostles, we are not denying any further history to the reality of revelation, which persists and advances in time; rather, with Christ and after him history was opened to God's infinite self-communication. History will introduce a new period bringing something different from what we now know — direct relation to God. This is also why the quasi-sacramental sign of this direct relation (the Church) continues to have a genuine history with real continuity and identity. Consequently, the temporal, historical character of salvation and revelation is not abolished by Christ; history's goal now is in Christ himself. But history still moves. This can be seen most clearly in the fact that there is not only a history of theology but also a history of dogmas. It is clear that the Church has a history, not merely in the sense that the Church is confronted with changing historical realities in the secular world, but because the nature of the Church itself has a history. In itself this history is no less significant than the history of revelation before Christ; it differs qualitatively, however, because it moves in the eschatological domain. God's offer of salvation and self-communication prevails throughout human history but within it. The Church was founded once and for all by Jesus Christ as an historical reality; in the theme of that history the Church gradually achieves its own identity. History of dogma, of structure, of spirituality, of heresy are partial elements of the history of the Church itself.

The Church, which is based on human being and becoming, cannot dispense with the genuinely temporal, historical character of man. The Church *is* by becoming. The Church becomes because it exists and exists only by becoming. The Church has a certain definite, essential beginning, but it attains its full identity only in the course of the process of becoming.

The temporal, historical character of the Church's action is of the utmost importance to pastoral theology. Authentic history is incumbent on the Church, which can find and perfectly fulfill itself only in the totality of its history. On this basis certain conclusions regarding the nature of pastoral theology can be drawn. Pastoral theology does not derive a knowledge of the living Church only from an abstract doctrine of the Church's nature;[15] it also observes the concrete forms the Church must take. As it observes the Church's detailed activity, pastoral theology exercises a critical function, judging the action of the Church in Eng-

[15] A dogmatic ecclesiology of the Church's essence presupposes the development of ecclesiology in the history of dogma and includes it in theoretical ecclesiology. The history of dogma in the field of ecclesiology does not take place, however, simply as a history of thought, but as the concrete history of the Church with its constitution, apostolate, encounter with the world. Consequently a dogmatic ecclesiology of the Church's essence already contains in fact the actual reality of the history of the Church. But it nevertheless remains true that pastoral theology itself must decide whether dogmatic ecclesiology has given sufficient attention to the concrete activity of the Church in history. And in this it will be forced to note that dogmatic ecclesiology in many respects does not do so sufficiently, even in those respects in which by its very nature it should (i.e., What is a bishop? a diocese? What is the theological foundation of a patriarchate? etc.).

land, New Zealand or the United States in the light of a dogmatic conception of the Church. Pastoral theology proceeds from knowledge of the Church's divinely established beginning to an experience of the dialectic and contradictions which appear in the concrete life of the Church and point beyond themselves to a fuller realization of its nature. As a regulative study for the building up of tomorrow's Church, pastoral theology can never lapse into a statistical and analytic sociology, a dogmatic ecclesiology of the Church's essence, a Canon Law, a theoretical moral and ascetical theology, a religious pedagogy, or a psychology of the pastoral care of souls. For what will be genuinely historical tomorrow cannot be deduced from the knowledge of today: pastoral prescriptions for the future can never be transformed into the maxims of an analytical science. In formulating maxims regarding the future life and action of the Church, to the extent that it goes beyond what can be deduced from dogmatic ecclesiology and from a methodical, sociological, and theological analysis of the present time, practical theology itself becomes free evaluation, decision, a part of the free historical activity of the Church and, if the conclusion is correct, a piece of prophecy, a charismatic summons from the future as God wills it. Complete separation between theology as a scientific branch of study and as decision or prophecy is impossible for historical man, who can never step outside the course of his own history. But awareness of the danger can serve to instill modesty into this study and the demands it expresses.

THE CHURCH: BASIS OF PASTORAL ACTION

6. Reconciliation of the Permanent and the Historical

The Church is always aware of its abiding nature, its right from Christ to exist. Every decision reflects to some extent this nature, which is the norm and limit of all decision. It would be theological rationalism alien to history to claim that the Church can reflect on its nature without looking at itself as historically conditioned. In this type of reflection, however, the nature in itself can never be wholly distinguished from its concrete embodiment. The nature of the Church is known in its new, historically emerging forms. The historical form of a personal essence is always unique and underivative, because it is free and historically individual (even in the temporal form it assumes). The correct proportion between maintaining the old and actualizing the new Church is something which can never come only from reflective analysis. Pastoral theology is, therefore, a study which approaches its object but never fully grasps it. At the same time it inevitably and often against its will attempts to provide a charismatic prescription. Practical theology — the result of tension between the old and the new — needs more than the abstract concepts of theology; it must call on the charismatic "instinct" of all members of the Church and its government. At the same time pastoral theology receives a summons to trust God's Spirit who assists the Church at that precise point where it can no longer reach certainty about its decisions.

4. *Differentiation in the Church: Laity and Hierarchy*

There is a fundamental material distinction within the one Church: on the one hand are the people of God as a whole; and on the other hand are those Christians who bear special powers bestowed on them by Christ for the service of his people — powers not possessed by every member of that holy people.

The individual human being is redeemed as a member of mankind, the human family. Despite the uniqueness of human freedom, man is necessarily a member of a community and society. The bestowal of grace on humanity and on the individual by God's self-giving action is not simply an event transcending the history of the individual and of mankind. The bestowal itself was to have, and has had a history of historical and social reflection, culminating in Jesus Christ. The reflex historical and social factors in the bestowal of grace on mankind constitute the Church. This social realization of the grace-endowed nature of man requires social order and direction and a moral and legal authority to make decisions concerning the action of all members of the society. For even in the sphere of redemptive history an anarchistic conception of society is self-destructive because salvation would no longer be present historically and socially. Anarchy fails to recognize man's social character at the innermost center of his personal life. The *formal* Catholic conception of hierarchical ministry in the Church is that official authority is not merely a necessary consequence of the social character of salvation, but that this ministry was determined by the founder of the Church

59

as regards its first bearers and its fundamental structures, which have to be handed on, not just reconstructed.[16]

Some principles must be formulated regarding the relation between office and office-holder and also between the members of the people of God who hold office and those who hold none. These principles are of special importance for pastoral theology. Church and hierarchy are not identical. The Church is the community of all baptized Christians who live in the confession of the same true faith in communion with the pastors authorized by Christ. Christians are not the *object* of the Church, but as community and society they *are the Church* itself (the organized Church, of course). As individuals they are the "object of service and concern" of the hierarchy. If it might be said of the individual Christian that he is the "object" of the Church (and not only its member), then he is not the object of the hierarchy alone but of the whole Body of Christ, for all Christians contribute to the salvation of one another.

Office and function are not identical; nor are vocation and authorization of a member in and for the Church. Baptism, confirmation, matrimony, orders (powers and services) are sacramentally bestowed and consecrated. Every charismatic endowment of a human being by God involves a commission and service in the Church. In principle there is no justified person in the Church who to some

[16] The decisive difference between the Catholic conception of ministry in the Church and that of Lutheran theology probably depends on whether the Church is regarded as a foundation from above and on whether we are convinced that it is God's will for there to be official ministry in the Church.

degree and in some direction has not such a charismatic gift. Every Christian possesses the seven gifts of the Holy Spirit. As a unique person each has his justifying grace as an expression of love addressed personally to him by his God, and therefore a supernatural, grace-given power to live his own unique life. In each instance this grace implies a special charism. Unique personal existence, achieved by grace (or lost), also involves a unique contribution to the being and activity of the Church, in other words, *a charism concerning the Church*.[17] If the Church is a sign urging belief by its whole reality — its holiness, its proclamation of God's love for the created and sinful world — it is clear that in this respect every Christian by his life in grace has a function in and for the Church. As a commission imposed by baptism, confirmation and matrimony, such a role is a lasting one, constitutive of the life of the Christian and of the Church, a vocation establishing a certain "calling" or profession. Ecclesiastical office in the strict sense must be seen within this general vocation and authorization for all Christians; it contributes to the specific activity of the Church, building it up. In the Church's social domain it compromises certain powers and rights which cannot belong to everyone because they involve obligations toward others and are expressly reserved to definite members of the ecclesiastical community and society.[18]

---

[17] It becomes clear in this way that *gratia gratum faciens* and *gratia gratis data* can denote two aspects of one and the same reality.

[18] This principle does not of course mean that it is possible rigorously to deduce from it what must remain the prerogative of the hierarchy and what must not. It would be difficult, for example, to indicate an *a*

The structure of the Church is not merely hierarchical. There is also the free, charismatic gift of the Spirit in the Church, and this must be respected by the Church's ministry. The official ministry must recognize that the Church lives and grows precisely as Church through the fulfillment of grace-given vocations and endowments which are not bestowed and transmitted sacramentally or in a legally regulated way but come directly "from above". These free charisms must account for themselves to the Church's hierarchy when they make demands which concern the life of the Church itself as a sacred society. The initiative of all Church life, however, cannot come from the hierarchy alone. Charism does not owe its ecclesial character to hierarchical blessing. There is Church where the Spirit is, where he ensures by his own eschatological, victorious power that he is acknowledged.

An office-holder, by the very fact of being a Christian, is also a bearer of charismatic possibilities; his grace of office (in contradistinction to his official authority) is a divine promise of a help which, sanctifying him and at the same time representing a charism for the Church, enables him to use his official powers for his own salvation and the salvation of others. This does not depend solely on the application of legitimate official powers. The best situation is, of course, when office and free spiritual gifts are combined in one person. An office-bearer should not relieve his burden by appealing to his official authority, but should try to win

priori principle from which it evidently follows that a non-baptized person can validly baptize. But the principle stated does throw light on the general *a priori* possibility of ministry in the Church.

people over to his authority through the testimony of the grace and power manifest in him. In the Church there are never human beings who are either exclusively bearers of office or of charism. Each bearer of office must work with his personal charism if he is not to be at variance with his office. God's victorious grace ensures that in the Church as a whole no absolute contradiction intervenes between office and charism or personal holiness, although history shows that it has occurred. The fact that sacramental grace-giving powers belong to the official ministry by the very nature of the Church proves that the official element in the Church is quite definitely pneumatic. "Official" does not mean something juxtaposed to spirit, charism and personal existence, but signifies a definite way in which the Holy Spirit and personal decision become present in the Church.

Not everything in the Church, even what belongs to it essentially, can be official, and this is explained by personal lives subject to time: not every human action engages the whole of life. It is also due to the uniqueness of individual persons: it is they after all who in different ways belong to the Church. Finally we see the difference between the eschatological victorious Church as a whole, fundamentally important for the individual's salvation, and the individual working out his salvation in "fear and trembling". Within the Church there is always preserved a domain proper to private Christian personal life, an area which can no longer tangibly (i.e., officially) be provided for by the Church.

CHAPTER TWO

Christians: Action in the Church

Pastoral theology describes the relation between normative principles and the Church's daily life in which its nature is actualized and made present in the historical situation of the moment. Since the Church is a socially organized community of men, the question inevitably arises: Who in this community performs the specific actions of the Church? For a community and society can act only through the concrete members of the community. Are all members of the Church capable of pastoral action? If so, are they all equal and do they hold the same mission, or is it the nature of the Church that different roles be given to each member?

In the history of pastoral theology it has been regarded as a self-evident axiom that the hierarchy alone is responsible for the Church's pastoral action; the laity at most share in this activity, but only in so far as they are called in as helpers by the hierarchy. If this concept were correct, the Church would be at least partially divided, i.e., the Church as hierarchy would be a channel of salvation and the Church composed of hierarchy and laity together would be the gift of salvation. The laity would be only the object of the Church's action, and pastoral theology — the Church reflecting on its own activity in the contemporary situation so as to lay down some guiding principles — would be a study of the activity of the hierarchy.

If, however, each member of the Church is acknowledged personal responsibility for its pastoral action, and if the constitution of the Church as gift of salvation and the action of the Church as instrument of salvation are understood as inseparable aspects of one reality — even then it does not follow that every member of the Church has the same kind of role in its pastoral life. Despite the identity of task and function which belongs to all members of the Church in virtue of their fundamentally equal membership, the question arises whether there are not specifically different functions in relation to the actualization of the Church and, if so, what the differences are in terms of the nature of the Church. If there are any essentially different roles, it means that Christians are capable of performing different kinds of services within the Church's pastorale.

1. The Whole Church

If all baptized persons (under the various conditions which need not be developed here) are members of the Church, it is evident that all are active members and therefore able to take part in the Church's specific activity. The term, "member of a body", which is used by Scripture to denote every Christian, would lose its meaning if there were members of the Church who were so only to the extent of being the object of the salvific activity of others. The Church is and lives by what all of its members *together* are and do.

But this is an obvious ecclesiological truth. Our thesis is that all members of the Church take part in its instrumental saving action because every aspect of the whole being and action of the Church has significance as a channel of salvation: each Christian in all he does as a member of the Church works for the salvation of all other Christians and for the salvation of all men, insofar as the Church itself is of importance for the salvation of the world. Each member of the Church, therefore, shares in the Church as gift of salvation and in the same measure as channel of salvation.

This thesis is certainly contained in the New Testament. For Paul it is taken as a matter of course that every member of the body of Christ has a service to perform for the whole body and its growth. Every member of the Church has a gift peculiar to himself, and each of these gifts is bestowed for the common good of the whole Church. Each has the duty and possibility of "edifying" others; with Paul such edification is regarded as contributing to the edification of the *Church,* because he never loses sight of the fundamentally ecclesiological sense of the word. The one responsible for the Church's edification is the whole Church itself (Eph 4:16).

The Church has always held fast to this conviction, even when it was not preached and taught. Intercessory prayer, mutual instruction, admonition and consolation, mutual forgiveness (which, because it awakens trust in the forgiving grace of God, is not only a duty of the person forgiving but also brings salvation to the person forgiven), blessings of parents over their children — these and many other ways in which Christians' service of edification assumes tangible form testify to the Church's conviction that every member in the Body of Christ can and must serve as a channel of salvation for all others.

The ultimate reason why every justified person in the body of Christ has such a mission as channel of salvation is his union with Christ. The Christian can bear fruit only to the extent that he remains in Christ, the vine, and receives vital force from him. But this fruitfulness, the manifestation of the plenitude of life of the vine, Christ himself, is not (according to John 15) simply the personal salvation of the individual Christian for his own sake; it is the gift which Christ himself offers by his death (Jn 12:24) and which he gives to the disciples to bring (Jn 15:16) — that of bearing fruit for the salvation of others. Of course this sharing in Christ's role as mediator of salvation is only instrumental. Christ is not only the sole mediator between God and man; he is salvation itself.

The condition of being taken into service for the salvation of others, of *diakonia* and of being God's collaborator, is not found in the official life and work of the Church alone; it is within every Christian. Here we touch on a decisive element in a truly Catholic ecclesiology. The Church is not simply a gift of salvation, not just the community of faithful who receive God's salvation through Christ, as Protestant theology suggests. It is not a channel of grace only in its hierarchy, as a "clerical" distortion of Catholic doctrine proposes. Nor does it serve as a channel of salvation only in

67

CHRISTIANS: ACTION IN THE CHURCH

those of its members who are "perfect", as a spiritualizing tendency in the theology of the Eastern Church since Origen likes to think. Each member of the Church accepts his personal charism united with Christ and is important for the body of Christ as God's "collaborator" (1 Cor 3:9; Col 4:11; 3 Jn 8, etc.).

2. Each Member of the Church

Each member of the Church actively shares in building up the Church — conveying grace to individual human beings. This does not mean that each Christian's role in the Church's self-realization is the same. Scripture testifies to the opposite: each person receives from Christ his own gift and task by which he contributes to the redemptive construction of the Church.

The differentiation of these missions is very elaborate and cannot be deduced from one single point of view. The gift which each Christian receives is for many reasons uniquely personal and individual. The various gifts all have, however, an intrinsic, essential common feature: they ultimately derive from the same union of the faithful with Christ, and even in their variety they are the gift of one and the same Spirit, as Paul emphasizes. They also ultimately serve as channels of the same redemption. Whatever the differences between them, and however differently they may be classified theologically, existentially, and from the point of view of Canon Law, they all bear the character of the same total salvation, which each in its way seeks to transmit. Every individual Christian's gift and role embodies salvation in its entirety. Because each gift is given for the Church as a whole, all fundamental pastoral action is at the same time the basic structure of even the most modest of charisms (those coming from being a Christian, special charisms, or office in the Church). Any further articulation of missions must agree with this common characteristic of all Christians and their pastoral action. Hence the efficacy of each individual function depends on the existence and efficacy of all others. Religious truth, for example, is only really heard where it is also practised with love. The sacramental powers attain their purpose only if the recipients are prepared for them by efficacious graces, and these in most cases are mediated by persons who themselves hold no office. Sacramental word and the word of preaching mutually condition one another; all ritual and liturgy ultimately tends towards that service of God which takes place in ordinary everyday life.

The Christian pastorale is diversified in a great variety of ways, but without detriment to its ultimate unity. The sources and explanation of this differentiation ultimately spring from two factors taken in conjunction — the nature of salvation and the nature of man. They are so manifold and at the same time interconnected because what is involved are revelations of the infinite plenitude of the one God. It is impossible to try to systematically delineate them.

Fundamentally the charisms and vocations in the Church are as various as are men in individual temperament, character, and history. These differences explain the diversity in spiritual gifts, for none is without importance for the salvation of the individual and consequently for his mission in the Church. Individual Christians and their functions in the Church are therefore distinguished by the different elements which constitute man's salvation both in its unity and in its diversity: the aspects of the one salvation as truth and love; the gift which is God himself and the liberated power of self-surrender to God; individual and cosmic fulfillment. Roles are diversified by the various dimensions of man as a unique being belonging to a community in his transcendence and historically concrete circumstances; by the particular features of individuals according to sex, intelligence, education, financial condition, free self-determination; by a radical vocation from God which operates through all these factors yet is not a mere formula for their sum-total. Which charisms and missions actually follow from these sources of differentiation and the resulting differences between Christians cannot be described here. One fundamental difference must, however, be mentioned: that between office and free spiritual gift.

3. Office and Charism

Before trying to throw light on the distinction between office and charism, we must stress once more the essential solidarity of all Christians and their different gifts. (God's Spirit can also distribute such gifts to men who do not belong to the historically visible Church yet whose Spirit-inspired gift may nevertheless be of importance for the Church.) In accordance with the incarnational principle of sacred history, the Church is a quasi-sacramental unity of Spirit and historical, visible embodiment; consequently, all action of the Church is determined by this basic structure. The free spiritual gifts, which are not susceptible of institutional regulation, are always those of baptized persons who profess one common faith within the Church (even as a human, social organization), who fit into the socially organized unity of the Church's life, and who place even their freest and most personal charism at the service of this Church. Conversely, all official authority is authority *within* the Church, not over the Church; it is necessarily based on that Christian character which the office-holder shares with all members of the Church. Despite its origin in a commission from on high, its nature is such that it can only be exercised within a Church which as a whole is animated by the Spirit of God. Only in this manner and through the operation of the free spiritual gifts which it implies can the Church receive guidance by official powers.

The individual office-holder can exercise his official powers in the concrete only if he too possesses a certain measure of the gift of the Spirit. For even those powers which operate sacramentally *ex opere operato* can have this kind of efficacy only if they are freely applied and find a suitable recipient. Both conditions of the *factual* occurrence of an *opus operatum* ultimately depend on free spiritual gifts, at least if these are understood in the comprehensive sense of God's grace-action, which remains free and cannot be institutionally administered by man. Ultimately, of course, the nature of the Church as eschatological redemptive community in contradistinction to the synagogue and other pre-Christian historical manifestations of divine salvation, consists precisely in the fact that the unity between divine grace and its empirical embodiment can no longer be broken. If this is understood, the fundamental unity of all divine saving activity in regard to and in the Church has been grasped, including all legitimate and essential differences between the various charisms and their recipients. In the New Covenant God's grace cannot act without relation to the Church. The eschatological promise that it will never lack the Spirit has been given to the ecclesial institution as a whole. This does not mean that the difference between office and free charism has become indistinct: within the social dimension of the Church (and therefore within the dimension of the sacramental sign and of the official word and law which bind the Church) a clear line of demarcation is indispensable. Nevertheless, office and charism belong so closely together that one cannot exist without the other, and despite their differences the two are interdependent.

Having established these conditions and reservations, we can now examine the difference between office and free charism, because only in that way can the character, differences, and solidarity of all Christians in the Church's pastoral action be clear. We say *free* charism because biblically and in fact the authorities of the Church's ministry are gifts of God's grace, not only because they are given by a free and unmerited award of God, but also because official authority by its nature aims at the sanctification of the members of the Church; for the holders of office it also implies a requirement and promise of their own sanctification, even when the office is exercised (validly and fruitfully) by a sinner.

The fact of such a distinction cannot be disputed in a Catholic ecclesiology. On the one hand, office exists in the Church as a permanent commission from Christ, and this commission becomes manifest in the historical and juridical order (imposition of hands and apostolic succession). The efficacy of this role is assured by the legitimacy of the commission. On the other hand, throughout the Church there are operations of God's Spirit in individual believers quite beyond the reach of man himself; they cannot be foreseen or organized by the official authorities and are not attainable by the administration of the sacraments alone, and yet they appear in the Church in the most varied forms and intensity. The existence of a divine-right hierarchy with powers which do not belong to every baptized person is a defined doctrine of faith (Denz. 359, 498, 853, 960, 966, 967, 1502, 1822). It can certainly also be regarded as an undoubted doctrine of the ordinary magisterium that there are actions of grace of the Spirit — not only in the Church (for the salvation of the individual himself) but also for the Church — which are different from these official powers and their use. Since both are vital parts of the Church, a pastoral theologian must mark out both areas of inquiry.

To further clarify the nature of office and free charism and to see the intimate connection between the two orders of gifts, it is not sufficient to take as a starting-point the idea of legal distribution of definite powers by those who are in evident possession of them. It is not sufficient even if we accept the possession of these powers as permanent and their transmission as taking place in forms established once and for all, socially visible and juridically verifiable. However indispensable that idea may be for the concept of office in the Church, its insufficiency as a cornerstone for pastoral theology can be shown on two grounds. In the first place, it does not make clear what distinguishes office in the Church from office in the synagogue or from divinely authorized office in secular society. At most it would be possible to explain their difference in material content, but not their formal structural difference. Second, why are there free charisms in and for the Church? It might be thought that all missions in the Church could be based on official appointment, if Church offices were constituted simply by a formal commission to perform a definite function in and for ecclesiastical society. These offices are *ultimately constituted* by a mission with which certain men are charged by Christ, receiving from him definite powers and rights in relation to other men; but Church office derives its character from the fact that it is office in the *Church:* it is what it is because of the nature of the Church itself. This character is best seen if we consider such office in its highest functions, as infallible magisterium and administration of the sacraments *ex opere operato,* and ask why an official ministry of precisely this kind exists.

In pre-Christian sacred history no such ministry did exist, for there were no sacraments in this sense and no teaching office as opposed to non-institutionalized prophecy. Yet, at least in the legitimate religion of the Old Testament, there was a divinely authorized ministry of kings and priests. The specific character of office in the New Testament is

74

undoubtedly drawn from the eschatological character of the Church. The Church in the New Testament is the abiding presence of Christ, both as fruit of redemption and as its instrument. In Christ alone, however, is there inseparable incarnational unity of God and man, grace and its visible historical manifestation. Because of the unmixed and inseparable unity of the divine and human in Christ, there is a similar unity in the presence of Christ which is the Church.

There is indefectibility in the Church wherever it commits itself absolutely as the presence of Christ in the world; there is an indefectible ministry in teaching, in the conferring of grace, and in the rest of the Church's activity; this ministry, this pastoral action belongs to the character of the Church. Because the Church is a society it necessarily possesses an official authority, but because it is a society which is the eschatological presence of Christ's redemption, it has an official authority which under certain conditions is indefectible by a special help from Christ. If Church authority were like legitimate human authority, it could be founded "from below" and given backing by divine authority; yet it would remain mutable and defectible. The Church's office, however, is founded by God precisely to help the Church represent the incarnational truth and grace of Christ in the world. To the extent that the ministry originates in this way, it is indefectible by nature. Conversely, the Church's ministry is of divine law only to the extent that it represents this indefectible presence of Christ and absolutely engages it in its action.

This does not mean that the exercise of office by divine

right is in every case either indefectible or not present at all. Because of the plurality of factors that constitute man and the Church, the particular activities of the official ministry form a unity of elements, each of which need not totally comprise the whole. This is analogous to man's freedom, which is not engaged to the same extent in every free act. Where pastoral action corresponding to the eschatological nature of the Church is involved, it is a ministry by divine right, indefectible, and implying total self-commitment by the Church. Where this is not the case — and that is often — we are dealing with free spiritual gifts, which by way of consequence are given some sort of institutional form.

The activity of the Church as a whole cannot be based solely on the official ministry; it requires completion by free charism and charismatics. No historical and temporal entity can realize its nature solely by those actions in which it commits itself totally: that would contradict its temporal, historical character. The Church is the pilgrim Church, still moving towards its perfect fulfillment. It possesses its own indefectible nature (as God's eschatological self-communication to mankind in Christ), but it possesses it in faith and hope and not by sight. If it were always to act indefectibly in every action, the Church would no longer be the temporal Church on pilgrimage in hope; the final Kingdom of God would have arrived. Nor does this mean that the operation of the Church is simply an extraneous mixture of indefectible and defectible actions. Both its eschatological indefectibility and its pilgrim existence must be at work in *all* the Church does. The occurrence of the freest of charisms is, therefore, a specifically ecclesial charism, and its character is co-determined by the nature of the indefectible Church. It is experienced and accepted in faith and hope and is an actuation of that grace which has been given irrevocably to the world in Christ and the Church. Conversely, the most official *opus operatum* and the most infallible doctrinal decision of the Church rest, for what they are really intended to signify, on free charism which cannot be officially organized. For the infallible promise of grace in a sacrament is only operative when non-sacramental grace produces its acceptance by the disposition it bestows, and the infallible doctrinal decision can only be rightly understood when it is heard in that grace and understanding of the faith which are no longer subject to official administration.

The Church's activity is based on the spiritual gifts of all its members because its pastorale takes place in faith, hope, and love beyond the scope of an official control. This charismatically grounded pastoral action has an official basis, is constitutive of office and even presupposes it, wherever the whole Church's action is really the eschatologically definitive presence of Christ in the world and in history. We can touch on the innermost metaphysical nature of ecclesial office only because its concrete reality has been experienced. Once the nature of that ministry has been explicitly realized *a posteriori* through experience, a practical norm for it can be drawn up in many cases from Scripture, doctrine and the practice of the Church.

4. The Church's One Office

Office in the Church, i.e., the authority to engage the entire Church in its own specific activity, is ultimately one, as is the indivisible nature of the Church. Office nevertheless comprises various elements, corresponding to the plurality of factors which make up that nature. The Church's practice and constitution show that its one ministry can be borne by a number of members participating in the pastorale in different ways. Each shares, however, in the single ministry of the one Church: every partial power and authority always refers to the totality of a single pastoral action and can only be rightly exercised in a living relation with the total authority.

Similarly, the individual Christian can use powers validly and morally only if he is united to the whole Church and to the corporate body of those who hold office. This is true not only of the power of jurisdiction but also of the power of order, which can, of course, be exercised validly in certain circumstances even if its holder is not fully united with the Church. But just as a baptized heretic and schismatic remains a true member of the Church, so too the heretical or schismatical bearer of a power of order is essentially linked to the Church by this power.

For pastoral theology it is very important to form a clear idea of how many Christians carry out the Church's one ministry. The question is not how can many people participate in the Church's office when it is identical in each — how, for example, is it possible to consecrate many bishops or priests? In such an ordination a particular power of jurisdiction or office, which by definition is already circumscribed, is given to a particular person. The question is rather how the particular offices with their different purposes originate from the single ministry as its branches. In answer it is often assumed that Christ himself, acting directly or through express commission to his apostles, established three degrees of the hierarchy — bishops, priests and deacons. Is this really the case?

The Church can confer its official power (provided its unity and plenitude remain represented in the Petrine office) in whole or in part in a way which seems to correspond to the need of the time. The fundamental way of transmitting office is sacramental ordination. The conferring of jurisdiction is a concrete specification of the Church's single power. The threefold hierarchy as regards the power of order is, therefore, by divine right because Church authority is itself by divine right, and also because its threefold articulation took place in apostolic times and is irreversible. Despite the *individual, personal nature* of official power, it demands *corporate exercise* by the episcopate, corresponding analogously to the relation between primacy and episcopate (another reason for the irreversibility of the hierarchy of deacon, priest and bishop). This exists only if the individual bishop has a circle of collaborators around him (priests and deacons taken as a corporate body, a unity among themselves). There are not priests just because the bishop needs collaborators and cannot do everything himself. That problem could be solved by increasing the number of bishops and restricting the extent of their territory, making every pastor a bishop. The reason is that despite the nature of an independent ("monarchical") power in each holder of office, he must have a council of advisors around him on the model of the archetype of all ecclesiastical authority: the apostolic college with Peter at its head. Even the Pope must never be without his senate, not merely as its executive but as its president, able to act independently, yet acting as head of the college even when acting "alone".

To illustrate what we have been saying, let us recall some relevant history and doctrine. The diaconate was established by the apostles themselves out of a pastoral necessity which arose unexpectedly. The content and scope of this "diaconate" of the seven followed quite simply from the immediate necessity of a division of labor in regard to the one apostolic function. The direction of the various churches in the apostolic age does not seem to have been the same everywhere: according to the locality, their rule seems either to have a more corporate or a more monarchical character (even though side by side with this single *episcopos,* at least in larger churches, there seems to have been an advisory council of collaborators, a *presbyterion*). The commission of those who were church leaders in the apostolic age seems to have been varied and rather fluid. This helps to explain the fluctuation in terminology denoting such offices, a flexibility mirroring an unfinished articulation of the various missions contained in the single ministry of the Church.

To take another example: priests of the Eastern Church administer confirmation as part of their normal apostolate. Western priests can validly administer confirmation with papal authorization. If we do not wish to regard the com-

munication of the power to confirm as taking place sud-
denly by a pure act of jurisdiction (whereas otherwise it
takes place through episcopal consecration), then the power
of the simple priest to confirm can be understood only as
the unbinding of a power already bestowed in principle
by sacerdotal ordination but bound in such a way that its
use is invalid. It is at least probable that the simple priest's
active power of ordaining to the priesthood is similar to
his power of confirming: he receives in principle at his own
ordination the sacramental power to raise others to the
priesthood, even though its exercise would be not only
illicit but invalid. The relation between the power of order
and the power of jurisdiction in the power to absolve sins
must presumably be understood in a similar way. The power
of jurisdiction which is exercised by a priest in giving
absolution is an intrinsic element of his power of order,
which can validly be exercised only if authorized by a higher
Church authority. This authorization is usually termed
"jurisdiction" and, not entirely correctly, identified with
the judicial power which the priest actively exercises in
giving absolution.

Similarly, it may be assumed that the bishop's actual
power of jurisdiction is given in episcopal ordination,
even though its valid exercise is only possible in accord
with the whole community of the Church, on the basis of
papal authorization. When we consider the difficulty in
drawing the distinction between priesthood and episcopacy
on the basis of the power of order, including fluctuations
of terminology, and when we give due consideration to
the power and importance of patriarchs and metropolitans

in the early centuries (not forgetting the nature of *chorepis-kopoi,* so difficult to distinguish in relation to bishop and priest) it is not at all easy to say that the "bishops" of the many very small churches in antiquity were in fact bishops, i.e., that they possessed that power of order and jurisdiction which today distinguishes the bishop from the priest. Apparently many men were called "bishop" because of imprecise, fluctuating use of words. Nor must it be over-looked that metropolitans, patriarchs and local synods attributed to themselves without contradiction a right and power over individual bishops for which no legal title was quoted at all. This right was evidently not regarded as needing to be established by a definite authority (the pope, for example); it must have been felt to have been merely a specification of the nature of the Church's ministry, in other words an *historical* form of the divine right.

The explanation of these historical facts and apparently several disparate doctrines can be expressed in these points:

1. The fundamental, original and universally regulative form (structure) of the Church's one power is the apostolic college with Peter at its head, competent to act personally. It follows that a bishop — a man who belongs to the collegiate senate of Peter and his successors, bearing the highest and full authority of the Church — together with his brother bishops and under Peter possesses all the power which exists in the Church, with the proviso that he is not the president of the college and cannot act as its representative. Moreover the bishop possesses his powers only to the extent that he is a member of that college. In power of order the

bishop is equal to the pope. The powers of sanctification in the Church belong to every bishop because they must be exercised everywhere. *The* Church must appear in every local Church, and the greatest celebration of the presence of redemption and of the Church itself, the Eucharist, must be found everywhere. Consequently, the powers which make possible such total presence of the Church in every locality cannot themselves be tied down geographically. Conversely, this makes it clear what a bishop is. However rightly a definite territory is assigned to him to make clear the power that is his in the maintenance of order in the Church, however right it is for him to be a local bishop, he is, nevertheless, first and foremost a member of the college of bishops, which exercises an essential and fundamental function in regard to the whole Church and to its personal head. In the theology of a bishop the local character of his episcopal powers must not be exaggerated, as the example of the apostles shows. When a man is called to be a member of the episcopal senate, he receives a sacramental call; such a call as a fundamental act of the nature of the Church is an *opus operatum*.

2. This single and complete authority of the bishop is a power of order and of jurisdiction which is conferred by his being sacramentally brought into the college of bishops. It is validly exercised to the extent that it is based on the irrevocable membership of the college, and it is known as episcopal power of order. From this one total power partial powers derive relating to the Church as a whole, i.e., its socially perceptible unity in space and time and its direct dependence on the pope, who represents the social

and visible unity of the Church. The valid exercise of these powers is connected with union with the pope and his consent and is the bishop's power of jurisdiction.

3. Corresponding to the monarchical-collegiate character of the papacy, the individual bishop should convoke a senate, a corporate body representing the plurality and variety of his flock. A bishop representing the Church in a particular local situation needs a corporate body of collaborators and advisers who can be given a share in his powers of order and jurisdiction in a variety of ways, analogous to the conferring of episcopal office itself.

5. The Bishop and the Diocese

In this chapter we have been considering how different Christians are responsible for the incarnation of the Church through its pastoral action. The ultimate responsibility lies with the whole Church — all Christians with the variety of their individual tasks. Along with the recipients of free charism are those who bear ecclesiastical office. That office is one, although its authority is borne by a multitude of persons with specifically different missions in the structure of the official ministry. First among the office-holders we must consider the bishop and his diocese. We begin with the episcopate and not with the papal primacy because the bishop is a minister of the Church who exists by divine right, and the college of bishops as a whole is the subject of the highest and most complete power of the Church in every respect. The description of the primacy as the principle of the unity of the episcopal college is best placed at the end of this chapter as its summary.

What is a bishop and what is a diocese? The two questions are closely linked and can only be answered together. We can define the bishop as the ruler of a diocese and a diocese as the area of the Church ruled by a bishop. At first glance this may seem to be nothing but a circular definition. A further description of the bishop as the bearer of certain powers of order does not solve that difficulty, however, for the question is precisely why are they possessed by a bishop and not by a priest? It seems probable that every priest has, at least in a "bound" manner, the same powers of order as a bishop, even if he cannot validly exercise them. *De facto* priests do not exercise the same powers of order as bishops, but that is hardly the definition of a bishop. A bishop cannot be defined in terms of powers of order if priests can in fact provide everything necessary for salvation, even the ordination of other priests. (It is also futile to define a bishop as a man who can consecrate another bishop because in a Church which is temporal and yet permanent the capability of transmitting office belongs to the very nature of office and in no way specifically distinguishes the bishop and his responsibilities.)

Furthermore, it is impossible to explain the nature of a diocese by a mere definition of the bishop on the basis of his powers of order alone, for then a diocese could only be defined as the local domain of someone regularly exercising episcopal power. Nothing is said about the size and character of a diocese as against smaller territorial or functional units in the Church. It would be quite easy, for example, to imagine a dean having all episcopal powers of order for his territory. If anyone objects that it would be inappropriate to split up the Church into such small units, then he is suggesting a new definition of a bishop on the basis of a diocese.

In other words, a bishop is the ruler of a diocese because a diocese must exist as a definite part of the Church with a definite size and character. A diocese must have a ruler, and the nature of a diocese would explain why certain powers of order should be reserved to its ruler. The problem of defining bishop and diocese shows that ultimately the bishop can be understood on the basis of the diocese, though a diocese is not definable in reference to a bishop.

We reach the same conclusion if we attempt to define the bishop in terms of his power of jurisdiction. It becomes highly problematic for many reasons, e.g., the fact that a vicar-general can possess the same power of jurisdiction without being a bishop. Like episcopal order, episcopal jurisdiction could refer to such small units in the Church that in practice every parish would be a diocese. This illustrates again that a diocese and a bishop cannot be explained by the formal nature of episcopal jurisdiction. Yet pastoral theology needs a definition of the diocese and the bishop which explains in principle what a diocese is as compared with a parish and shows why each must exist. Only then is there a criterion and practical norm for judging existing dioceses to see whether they correspond in structure and size to the nature of a diocese as it ought to be. The difficulty cannot be overcome by declaring that the bishop is defined by the possession of certain powers of order and jurisdiction in conjunction, for such a definition does not permit any objective grasp of the nature of a diocese.

To answer our question, therefore, we must start with the nature of the diocese. We must try to describe it in such a way that no appeal is made to the known attributes of a bishop but that it becomes clear why a diocese can meaningfully be ruled only by the authority of a bishop.

To make any progress with the question we must return to the theorem that the apostolic college and the college of bishops, in unity with Peter and the pope, hold the highest authority in the Church. Here the bishop can still in a certain sense be defined without recourse to a diocese. The Church as a whole needs a highest authority; according to the will of Christ, the bearer is not a single physical person but a corporate body under a president, who can also act personally in the name of the college without being commissioned to do so in a juridical act. The episcopal college, however, is incapable of juridical action without Peter and the pope. The college as a whole, with and under the pope, is actively responsible for the total government of the Church, even apart from a general council. Consequently, a bishop can be defined on the basis of his membership in the group which governs the whole Church. Such a role properly belongs to the bishop even prior to a special relationship to a particular part of the Church. Under certain conditions (which are not met by the wish to honor or promote ecclesiastical officials), it can be quite meaningful for someone to be a member of this highest ruling body of the Church without being a territorial bishop.

How does a bishop become a territorial bishop? This

amounts to asking why a particular bishop is assigned a particular territory to govern with certain definite powers to the exclusion of the other bishops. Also, which territory is appropriate to be ruled by a bishop? These questions are still concerns of theoretical ecclesiology; once it has discovered the general principles determining the nature of a diocese and consequently of an actual bishop, then it will be possible for pastoral theology to say what a diocese is and ought to be in the face of present-day social and historical situations.

First of all, it is clear that larger units in the Church need guidance: the larger the Church, the more extensive its territory, the more its constituent parts need a control which cannot be exercised directly by the highest governing body. The larger sections of the Church require a direct rule with the appointed holding corresponding powers. This is to say that immediate direction must be exercised by members of the highest governing body itself.

In the abstract we can conceive of the Church's central government as a sort of senate, a small episcopal body with the pope at its head; various parts of the Church would be ruled by "priests" with delegated powers. To judge such a possibility we only need think of the apparently strictly logical constitution of the "New Apostolic Church",[1] which has a supreme governing body of twelve, and only twelve,

[1] The New Apostolic Church is a German adventist sect dating from 1855. Its government is modeled closely upon the apostolic community described in the Scriptures. Today there are 400,000 members in Germany and 35,000 members in Switzerland with only scattered membership in other parts of the world.

"apostles". At first sight it might seem that this church could be deduced more logically from the structure of the apostolic Church or else that (as Lutheran ecclesiology generally affirms) it is impossible to deduce from the actual constitution of the apostolic Church any concrete guiding principles binding on later ages. The Catholic doctrine of the Church seems, in comparison with these two views, to occupy a rather unclear middle position. On the one hand, it firmly maintains that by divine law the apostolic college must have a successor holding the same powers as itself. On the other, it presents as the successor of the apostolic college a body which by its numbers and dispersion throughout the world and by the restriction of its individual members to a particular territory does not seem to have much in common with the apostles.

Why, then, is a member of the college of bishops a territorial bishop, or conversely, why is a territorial bishop not simply a deputy of the college of bishops?

According to the teaching of the New Testament there are members of the one Church which form its parts in such a way that in them the Church becomes present in the world at a certain point in space and time. Certain local congregations, i.e., parts of the Church, are themselves called "church", bearing the same name as the whole Church. In the New Testament this is not mere chance or imprecise terminology. The reason is that in each Christian the whole Church comes into action and is present in the world. In fact the whole can attain its greatest actuality and most intense historical presence only in the concrete spatio-temporal actions of its parts. This is shown most clearly in the celebration of the Eucharist: as a meal it necessarily has the character of an event tied to a particular point in space and time and can only be realized in a particular part of the Church. Yet it is the highest and most intense self-realization and actualized presence of the entire Church. It is always *simultaneously* the celebration of the local congregation and that of the whole Church, as is all other ecclesial pastoral action. From this we can deduce that a part of this kind of Church should be headed by a member of the Church's ruling body, that is, by a bishop.

In objection to our conclusions, it can be pointed out that following this reasoning the leader of every local liturgical community would have to be a bishop, i.e., a member of the body succeeding the apostolic college. First, we must admit that almost to the end of the patristic period this was more or less the case. The local liturgical community was presided over by a bishop with his presbyterium, and there was a bishop in all congregations which formed a really independent liturgical unit. We can say that to some extent bishop and pastor were then identical and that the priests were essentially curates and not the leaders of independent eucharistic communities. The objection, however, is ultimately false because it overlooks the fact that a church community does not make the whole Church present and carry out its pastorale *solely* by the fact that it can be an independent eucharistic assembly: the Eucharistic is not the only action of the Church.

To further precisely what we have said, every part of the Church in which the whole Church can act to a considerable extent in respect to all of its activities should be directed

by a member of Church's governing body. We can therefore say that a diocese is a portion of the Church in which
all that the Church is can find realization and be manifested
in a way proper to the particular diocese. We have immediately added "in a way proper to it" to this "definition" of the
diocese because it is evident from the teaching of the New
Testament that the Church does not consist of absolutely
homogenous parts but is an organically differentiated
structure. If this is true of all parts of the Church from the
greatest to the smallest, then the distinguishing mark of
the diocese is that, without prejudice to what belongs to it
individually, it actualizes in space and time the whole
nature of the Church in all its dimensions and functions.
This cannot be said of all of the smaller individual members
of the Church. If and to the extent, therefore, that a part
of the Church is itself "church", i.e., the territorial presence
of the whole Church, it must be ruled by a member of that
corporate body which represents and bears the Church's
authority. Conversely, where it cannot seriously be said
of a part of the Church that it is itself "church", it is mean-
ingless and inappropriate for it to be directed by a
bishop.

At this point in our reflections we can introduce another
consideration of the greatest importance for pastoral
theology. The college of bishops as the highest governing
body of the Church is of divine right, and for that reason
the episcopate, though not the bishop, is also of divine
right. In the nomination of a bishop to a see a juridical
element — ecclesiastical and human — supervenes on the
divine right of the episcopate as a corporate body. This

becomes clearer if we think of how the concrete form of the diocese has changed in regard to size, population, actual mode of administration, etc. This human legal element is not simply juxtaposed on the divine right of the episcopate but is its concrete, historical embodiment, the only way the divine right of the episcopate can be realized at all.

Taking into consideration what we have said about small territorial sections of the Church (dioceses), we see why the necessary guidance of major, supra-diocesan areas can be undertaken only by a member of the college of bishops. The same things may be said about the direction of a major section of the Church and the person responsible for it as can be said of the government of a diocese. Such large "churches" (patriarchates, metropolitan provinces, diocesan associations, which at the present time are seeking to form bishops' conferences equipped with power of jurisdiction in order to become really capable of action as major Church units) must not be regarded simply as administrative units in the Church. They can also have the character of a church and can be concrete entities which rightly call for rule by a bishop, whether he is called a metropolitan, patriarch, primate, president of a bishops' conference, etc. In view of this, the determination of the Eastern rite Catholics in the Near East to maintain and develop their patriarchal constitution is not stubborn opposition or nostalgia for the past. When it is clear that the nature of a diocese must be envisaged as a natural framework of human life forming a unit within the perspective of redemptive history, and that this makes it possible for the Church to be present and to realize its nature at least partially in all of its essential missions, then it is also apparent that larger natural and historical domains are not arbitrary divisions made by the Church's central administration. They truly constitute a "church" (the Australian Church, the American Church, etc.) in the same way as the church which we call a diocese. Large churches do not lower the individual dioceses contained in them to the rank of a deanery: a real diocese always retains the character of a church. Whether such a large unit is to be ruled by a single "great bishop" (archbishop, metropolitan, primate) or in a more corporate manner is a secondary matter; even corporate direction (e.g., by a bishops' conference) would not conceal the Church's ultimate structure, for a corporate body is analogous to the universal episcopate.

The following ideas are suggestions or possibilities for applying the fundamental principle of the nature of a diocese to the contemporary situation. A diocese is ultimately based on a natural fact: the geographical unity of a territory. Within the natural domain of the diocese a certain number of people live and certain natural conditions for community life must be present — legal, linguistic, political, communications. All these are the natural presuppositions of a diocese. Different natural conditions are, however, required today for a church to be able to represent *the* Church in a quite definite way. If today's diocese were like a diocese of the 4th century, for example, in regard to its life, administration, liturgy, possibilities of confrontation with its own intellectual situation, missionary possibilities, theology, etc., it would be no more than an historical image of the 4th-century Church.

Pastoral theology cannot apply its principles like strict calculus; a good deal of common sense and prudence are also involved, always taking into account the various historical developments which have taken place in the Church. A diocese of only some 10,000 people, for example, which cannot educate its clergy as clergy of a particular church, which is not able to confront the intellectual tendencies of the age, which cannot be the basis of the pastoral institutions of a supra-parochial kind which are required in the present day, and which is so small that it cannot have its own distinctive character in the Church — such a diocese is certainly not a part of the Church which should be ruled by a bishop. The representative of such a church can numerically swell the college of bishops into a throng of uniform ecclesiastical functionaries, but he cannot be a member of the corporate body in which each bishop is to represent one "tribe of Israel" among the many families of the people of God, and thereby the real multiplicity of the Church and the gifts of its members. It is of course not possible to lay down the number of square miles or inhabitants which would be obligatory for all dioceses throughout the world. But the existence of prefectures apostolic and vicariates shows that not every good-sized territorial area can be made into a diocese. Even where the governor of such a unit possesses practically all the powers of a bishop, he is not yet named a bishop because he is not the head of a church which could rightly be called a diocese. Conversely, there are only too clearly ecclesiastical administrative structures which were once churches but are no longer so today, although they still bear the name. They lack those general natural, human conditions which are required for a community to be called a church ruled by a successor of an apostle.

6. *The Presbyterium and the Individual Priest*

The diocese is the "local church", for only there is the Church really present in its various aspects and functions. This local church is and remains a unity; it exists to carry out the Church's one pastoral activity. The unity of the diocesan church demands that the parts which make it up be as varied as the life of the Church itself. A diocese is not one because everything in it is the same, nor is it merely a grouping of identical parishes. The territorial principle cannot be *the* fundamental and primary principle of the organization of a diocese. The diocese remains a unity which is prior to small territorial units and does not exist as their sum total. Consequently, the diocese has missions which need not always be carried out on the parish level. The bishop has a relationship to the entire diocese and all its members which is not mediated by parishes and priests. (The same thing is true of the relation between the bishop and a priest who is an assistant in a parish: it is not primarily mediated by their relation to the pastor.)

We saw earlier that the Church's supreme governing body consists by divine right of a dialectical unity of monarchical and collegiate principles. A consultative body surrounding a personal office-holder is, therefore, a reality which has profound roots in the divine formation of the Church. From the earliest days of the Church the bishop appears as an office-holder who is surrounded by a "presbyterium" as an advisory council. Sometimes this presbyterium was simply the bishop's advisory senate; in other instances there were communities which were ruled corporately so that the "bishop" had more the character of being first among equals. At all events, the irreversible constitutional history of the apostolic Church — a part of revelation itself — led to a monarchical episcopate which was always surrounded by a presbyterium. We can say, therefore, that history proves a bishop must always by divine right be surrounded by a presbyterium: administration of the Church solely by bishops with equal powers (under the pope), who each ruled a community without priests, would transgress the divine law of the Church. There are exceptions, of course, as in the case of an itinerant missionary bishop, but they only prove the rule.

Also, the presbyterium is logically and objectively prior to the individual priest. The bishop does not consecrate and authorize priests to help him only after he has tried to work alone and failed. What is primary and fundamental is the presbyterium, so that through it the individual priest has a relation to the bishop and to his whole pastorale. Even when the individual priest has a particular territory assigned to him as the official sphere of his work, he is a member of the presbyterium and has a task and responsibility to the diocese as a whole, obligations which are not satisfied by diligence in his particular post.

Obviously a bishop must entrust the members of his senate with various functions which belong to his office but which he cannot personally perform. According to the teaching of the Church there are priests together with non-sacerdotal "servers" (i. e., not appointed to lead the eucharistic celebration), subordinate to the bishop, who are his authorized collaborators *(ministri)*; therefore, the triple division of the Church's hierarchy into bishops, priests and servers (deacons) is declared to exist by divine right. It is clear that the bishop's delegates and assistants should be drawn from his advisory council since its members have a general responsibility for the whole diocese.[2]

Unlike the bishop, priest and deacon are not oriented toward a particular territory, as is evident in present-day Canon Law. A member of the college of bishops can have a direct jurisdictional commission only in regard to his own diocese, excluding all other bishops from this authority. A priest, on the contrary, although he is a member of a presbyterium, can exercise a function in the whole diocese without territorial restriction.

Participation in the bishop's office and powers is conferred for the same reasons that a bishop must give others a share in his responsibilities. This means he should not simply give a number of persons a share in his mission and power as a whole (as if, for example, he were to have an

---

[2] Sharing the official power of the bishop concerns and involves the Church and its pastorale. If a permanent and considerable share in this power is involved, then a participation in the sacramental mode of transmitting the one episcopal authority is implied, together with participation in the sacramental ordination of the bishop.

auxiliary bishop who was also his vicar general), but should hand over a certain portion of the episcopal functions and powers. The domains and activities of the Church are manifold, and the tasks of the hierarchy are correspondingly varied; since the bishop bears the plenitude of the Church's office, he has many functions which in principle should be entrusted to others separately and often only in various degrees. There is an objective reason why the bishop's many tasks and powers must be delegated: we shall call this monarchical-collegiate postulate the functional principle. Partial episcopal delegation can be permanent or temporary; it can relate to the power of order and so to the power of jurisdiction inherent in it and necessary for its practical exercise, or it can relate to the power of jurisdiction alone. Participation in the bishop's role in accordance with the functional principle can also be understood so that the delegation is limited to a particular group of persons or to a particular territory. The first we shall call the personal principle, the second we shall call the territorial principle of participation in the office of bishop.

On the basis of these three principles all kinds of participation in the episcopal mission can be explained. Where the bishop shares his essential role of presiding over the liturgical community of his church (and consequently the other powers of order which by tradition are inseparably connected with the priest-president of the liturgy), we have what we call a priest. The office of president of the liturgy is regarded as permanent by its nature and implies that it is a sacrament since the whole Church is engaged in conferring the office. If a bishop confers a share in his office of charitable service and *as a consequence* commissions a certain man to serve the bread of life (the Eucharist and the word of God) and to perform other services as a permanent office with sacramental ordination, he establishes the office of deacon.

By leading a liturgical community within the diocese the priest shares in only *one* of the bishop's functions, it is true, but he stands nearest to the *entire* mission of the bishop because the central mystery of the Church is realized in the celebration of the Eucharist. The priest is oriented toward this episcopal role because as a member of the presbyterium he contributes to the representation of the multiplicity of the people of God when the bishop celebrates the Eucharist, and also because he is able to conduct a celebration of the Eucharist himself. The priest receives the power to conduct the celebration of the Eucharist in the name of Christ and the Church because the reality and need of the "Church" for the Eucharist still exist where the bishop can no longer preside. He can entrust the offering of the Eucharist only to a member of his presbyterium.

It should be possible to celebrate the Eucharist both as the bond of love and as the sacrament of ecclesial community in groups of Christians who form smaller circles than the whole community united in an episcopal Church. The Eucharist has to be celebrated "in all places". This makes it clear that the functional principle, which requires the priest subordinate to the bishop as sharer in his functions, of itself implies both the personal and territorial principle. It opens the possibility of specifying more precisely the sacerdotal role and office, and so of making the priest responsible for the liturgy of a personal or territorial community of worshipers; the priesthood by its very essence is related to a community. At an "absolute ordination" (which now is the most common and which obscures the real nature of the priesthood) where a tangible relation to a personal or territorial community is no longer involved, the meaning of ordination and of the priesthood is lost.

This is not the place to give a detailed explanation of participation in episcopal office, even though the functional, personal and territorial principles help us to understand the most varied forms of the Church's ministry. On the same basis it is quite possible for other new forms of office to be created if they are called for by the ever-changing situation of the Church. What is immutable in all of the Church's new historical forms is that these offices are participations in the mission of the bishop and remain subordinate to him. Any participation of this kind must imply the power of offering the eucharistic sacrifice, although certain other sacramental powers of the bishop can be transmitted in conjunction with the specifically sacerdotal eucharistic power. This framework of divine law is ultimately built into the nature of the Church itself so that official powers can be transmitted in a great variety of combinations and degrees, as the age we live in demands.

7. The Parish

This study is not the place for a detailed analysis of the function, life, divisions and organizations of a parish. We

100

wish only briefly to apply to the parish our conclusions from theoretical ecclesiology. We should keep in mind that the parish is not simply a miniature diocese since within the diocese we find other equally important branches of the life of the Church. Nevertheless, the parish must be given special attention in our reflections since it does have the greatest resemblance to the diocese. It is based on the territorial principle, and in contrast to other infra-diocesan church organizations has the greatest number of different functions.

At the outset it must be noted that the diocese is not composed solely of parishes. According to present Canon Law, of course, the whole area of a diocese has to be divided into parishes so their sum does coincide with the diocesan territory. That does not mean, however, that all that belongs to the purpose and life of a diocese is identical with the total of its parishes. There is a functional as well as a personal principle of division of ecclesiastical ministry within the diocese, and both are prior to the territorial principle. In a diocese there are those who share in the bishop's mission by holding limited powers; yet they are not identical with the parish and should not be regarded as its auxiliaries. A personal parish — of students, actors, lawyers — can therefore have as much justification as a territorial parish. It can be an equally concrete embodiment of the function of the bishop and diocese; this kind of non-territorial community of worshipers united by personal and professional bonds can be of far greater Christian significance than the more artificial society created by the neighborhood in which the parishioners happen to live. Given the geographical circumstances of a diocese, the bishop can have extremely important and direct obligations which are impossible to fulfill on the basis of small individual parishes. The diocese has a vocation to represent and carry out the whole life of the Church in all its aspects, and this is impossible in small parishes.

A diocese must be more than the sum of its parishes plus the central administration. The relation of the Church to the state and the reaction of the Church to modern problems can find expression only in larger social and cultural organizations. The development of theology, the evolution of the church art, higher education, social works, training centres of various groups, trades and professions, the church press — these aspects of Christian life cannot find expression within the framework of the parish, nor can the parishes unite to realize them through subsidiary organizations. On the other hand such duties cannot be performed by the bishop's central office or by the bishop alone. If special organizations are created, they spring just as directly from the nature of the diocese as do the parishes. The same relation that holds between branches of diocesan life and the parishes also exists between the persons who administer them and the pastors. The former cannot be auxiliaries of the latter as though the same curate were shared by several pastors. The precise relationship between these permanent diocesan organizations and parochial organizations is one which is continually changing and cannot be deduced once and for all from the nature of the Church.

In the age of small population the simplicity of social

conditions and the difficulties of travel explained why land was the basis of the whole life of the individual; it was natural for the territorial principle to be almost the only one for the division of the Church and its ministry. This error was always contested, however, by the existence of the itinerant prophets of the post-apostolic Church, the institution of the *chorepiskopoi,* the pastoral activities of exempt mendicant orders, the church schools and press, the church life of personal associations such as Third Orders, guilds, and since the 19th century professional organizations and confraternities. The territorial principle can never be the sole foundation of the parish, just as it can never be the only foundation of a diocese.

What is the positive function of the parish? We must recall that the accomplishment of the highest mystery of the Church, the celebration of the Eucharist, is linked to a place, that it occurs "in all places", that the bishop's altar cannot be the only one in the diocese, and finally that even in the future the territorial, local congregation will be the normal type of liturgical assembly. The local liturgical congregation is the essence of a parish; the parish should therefore be defined in terms of it. We have already said that there can be other liturgical communities in addition to and in subordination to that of the bishop and that they are just as fundamental as the territorial congregations. A monastic community, for example, forms a liturgical assembly which cannot be regarded as a convenient auxiliary to a parish, nor is it based on the fact that the members of the monastic community live in one place. Yet since the Eucharist cannot be celebrated unless a number of people come together in the same place, the most normal situation is for those Christians who live together in the same neighborhood to come together at the same altar. The social and individual significance of living together in a local community has no doubt been very different at different times. In today's urban society locale is much less important because home, place of work, centers of social life, of leisure activities, of culture, etc., are becoming increasingly independent of one another. The proximity of homes which may be little more than places to eat and sleep is not at all the same thing as the home environment of villages and small towns which used to form the natural liturgical community. Yet even today physical neighborhood still has human, personal significance, and for our celebration of the Eucharist on weekday mornings or evenings and on Sundays and holy days it is normally the almost indispensable natural condition of a community of worshipers.

It is difficult to conceive any other basis for the meaning and necessity of a parish than this local liturgical congregation drawn from the same neighborhood. The nature and function of a parish only extend, therefore, as far as can be justified by this point of view. It is not possible to say, for example, that because a parish exists it *must* have a school within its boundaries. Such an argument presupposes that the parishioners form a sociological group; as a consequence they can aim at a specific formation and education for the children — the future parishioners — based on the framework of the parish. Such a conclusion cannot be drawn from the nature of a parish if social changes have moved schools out of the milieu which still forms the liturgical community. In that case it can be questioned whether the pastor is the best teacher for the children who live in his particular area but who do not go to school there.

As far as it is possible to talk of the permanent nature of a parish at all, i.e., as far as the geographical neighborhood also forms the liturgical community, the nature of the parish can include only a community and its strictly *theological* consequences. For example, one of the functions of the pastor will be that proclamation of the word of God which is an integral part of the celebration of the Eucharist. The practical Christian activity which radiates from the celebration of the unity of the Church in the Eucharist — to the extent that it finds its natural expression in terms of a particular neighborhood and yet calls for some institutional form — will also be a task for the parish precisely because it is a local liturgical community. A parish will have the right and duty to create the conditions of a well-ordered liturgical community. Its leader must know which Christians ought to belong to it. Since even today the local congregation is the normal and the most important framework for the new generation, the parish priest will have to educate the young people in his parish as well as their parents. Certainly he also has a mission to the people within his parish who are not yet Catholics or who no longer live their faith.

From what has been said it follows that the parish and the role of the pastor must be determined from the point of view of the altar. As opposed to the theology of the pastor which demands that he do anything and everything in his parish which is the work of the Church, we believe that what cannot be derived from the altar cannot be the respon-

CHRISTIANS: ACTION IN THE CHURCH

sibility of the parish and the pastor (and there are such things, for the whole pastorale of the Church cannot be inferred from the Eucharist). Other institutions must be formed by the diocese for such purposes. It is another question how far such things can also be managed by the pastor acting in a double capacity: the genuine parish tasks are his chief concern, and everything else takes second place.

8. *The Diaconate and the Deacon*

The Council of Trent defined that the hierarchy consists not only of bishops and priests but also of "ministers", who must be deacons within the immutable, divinely established structure of the Church. Sacramentally ordained deacons who are not priests have not played any great part in the practical life of the Western Church. That does not prove, however, that the office no longer exists or that it is insignificant for the concrete life of the Church. If properly analyzed, history shows only that the diaconal function is seldom conferred by sacramental ordination. A serious investigation of the decree on the restoration of the diaconate is beyond the scope of this study, but we do need to see that this office exists in the Western Church. If we realize that a sacramental ordination exists for the sake of the required office and not vice versa, it is easy to see that the office does exist, even if the Church usually confers the sacramental initiation to it only on men who do not exercise it except in conjunction with their priestly office. Because of the nature of the Church's pastorale and the exigencies of the historical situation the Church officially and permanently

106

assigns men functions and corresponding powers which do not have a specifically sacerdotal character but nevertheless belong to the hierarchy's and especially to the bishop's role. There are unordained men who are professionally and permanently in the service of the teaching Church, or who professionally and officially perform the charitable works which belong to the hierarchy; there are others who possess higher functions in the administration of the Church or even take over ministerial functions in divine worship. All such services, if performed permanently and professionally, can certainly be called diaconal functions, once we get rid of the idea that they can only be conferred by sacramental ordination. This is a false idea, if for no other reason than the fact that even the traditional deacon's duties can be performed by an unordained man with the proper authorization. The diaconal office does not have to simultaneously comprise all the functions which are usually listed as those of sacramentally ordained deacons since the Church could undoubtedly ordain a man deacon without giving him the right to preach or to distribute Communion.

We can therefore draw an axiom from the traditional teaching about the three grades of holy orders and their graded power of jurisdiction: in the Church there should be offices and bearers of official functions separate from the priesthood and priest. Though undeniable this axiom has been disregarded in the Church for many hundreds of years. Even the recent emphasis on the role of the layman and of the lay apostolate has not shaken the widespread belief that pastoral action is either the domain of the priest alone or of the laity only insofar as they "share" in the apostolate of the hierarchy. To a large extent it is tacitly assumed that laymen who are professionally and permanently in the service of the Church are *ipso facto* auxiliaries of the pastor. However, the Church's one mission found in its fulness in the bishop is divided into a sacerdotal and a diaconal office by divine law and not simply because a pastor needs help in his work; it is clear then that the diaconate stands in direct relation to the episcopate and is not mediated by the sacerdotal office. Thus the importance of the diaconate in patristic times, *side by side* with the presbyterium, cannot be dismissed as an anomaly of the times. A diaconal office under the bishop and in a certain respect side by side with the presbyterium belongs to the essential structure of the Church and is represented by Christians who are neither bishops nor priests.

Because this theology of the diaconate is now much more widely accepted, a more contemporary development of this necessary office is being worked out, for the Church is once again going to confer the higher grades of the diaconate by sacramental ordination.[3] In the tangible manner of a sacrament this assures Christians of that grace of office which is already offered them by the Church's call to service. Where an official function of a supraparochial kind seems necessary for the diocese but is not necessarily connected

[3] Josef Hornef, a peritus at Vatican II, has spent his career as a lay theologian developing a theology of the diaconate and was closely connected with the Council's document on the diaconate. A fine summary of his work as applied to the English speaking churches is available in his article, "The Lay Diaconate for America?" in *Listening* (Spring, 1967).

with the direction of a congregation of worshipers, it should be entrusted to a deacon, who is a "minister of the bishop" and not a parish priest's assistant.

These considerations apply particularly where there is a shortage of priests. Such a scarcity is often not a real lack of priests to preside over liturgical communities but is only an apparent shortage because it is taken for granted that ecclesial activity can be adequately carried out only by priests. Also, the reasons put forward for priestly celibacy cannot be directly applied to bearers of a non-sacerdotal office even if it is bestowed by sacramental ordination. If there are reasons for celibacy, they must be found in the office itself and not in the sacramental rite which confers it.

9. The Pope and the Roman Central Government

Among those responsible for the Church's pastoral activity the pope and the papal officials belong together but are too important to be treated under a single heading. It is obviously necessary for the pope to make use of auxiliaries who can develop their own initiative, but it is also evident that certain decisive functions of the pope, particularly of a doctrinal kind, are intrinsically impossible to delegate. What was said earlier about the relation between the Church's office and the Church itself and between office and free charism applies in every respect to the papacy. The papacy is not identical with the Church and is not called upon to administer and direct all the free spiritual gifts in the Church, although it must test charisms and maintain them in the unity of faith and love. Even the papacy has a merely ministerial function in relation to the Spirit, who manifests himself only in the whole Church. Without detriment to the juridical unity of the Church with its juridical and historical centre in the papacy, the Church is a manifold system which has its sole sovereign unity in the Spirit of God himself.

The doctrine of the papacy and its officials as deputies of the Church's life forms an indispensable part of a pastoral theology which tries to be a normative study of the actual functioning of the Church in all its spheres. Pastoral theology cannot assume that what it has to say about papacy and curia is already stated in dogmatic ecclesiology or in Canon Law. Dogmatic ecclesiology limits itself to the universal principles governing the pope's primacy of jurisdiction and his infallible magisterium, and Canon Law deals almost exclusively with what is, not with what ought to be. The nature and role of the papacy cannot be grasped from purely juridical points of view. Because of the total lack of any preparatory works of genuine pastoral theology on the topic, it is possible here to reflect only briefly on a few dogmatic principles significant for a pastoral theology of the papacy as the highest instrument of the Church's saving action, and to undertake a few reflections on the interpretation to be given to the central ecclesial government.

It may be noted in passing that pastoral theology can treat of the nature and function of ecumenical councils. Council and pope are both bearers of the complete authority of the Church, so that much that has to be said concerning the pope also applies to the general council. As representing the universal episcopate, a council has possibilities and tasks which are quite different from those of the pope. The scope of *Studies in Pastoral Theology* is limited, however, and so we mention the ecumenical council only as an indication of the many areas still almost untouched by pastoral theologians.

1. The Pope

The successor of St. Peter as bishop of Rome holds the complete, immediate, highest episcopal jurisdiction over the whole Church — all dioceses and all bishops. In terms of pastoral theology what does this mean? In the public life of the Church as well as in the life of the individual Christian everything is radically encompassed by the primacy of papal jurisdictional power. In principle this power relates to everything belonging to the visible, concrete Church and to the Spirit who finds objective incarnational and ecclesial expression. Papal power is related to the faith, hope, love and grace of the individual, but that does not mean that everything in the Church proceeds under the papacy's juridical forms of action. Because the episcopate exists by divine right, unofficial vital movements thrive in the Church without coming into contact with the exercise of the universal primacy. Neither bishops nor faithful may regard themselves as mere executors of papal instructions. It would be wrong if all initiative began with the Holy See and passive obedience to the Pope were proposed as a goal of Christian life. Everything which happens in the Church can be subsumed, however, under the formal principle which the Holy See proclaims since all of the Church's pastoral

111

action is a living realization of this belief, hope and love preached above all by the pope. Still the Church is the Body of Christ and the pope exercises only a particular role of service within the Church.

The positive meaning of this authority which is universal and yet is not the source and driving-force of everything in the Church can only be that of representing and guaranteeing the unity of the Church, established and preserved by the Spirit of God. The papacy is not the only principle of ecclesial unity since the Eucharist and Scripture with its normative character for the whole of Christian belief have unifying functions in the community of faith. The papacy can, therefore, be termed the principle of the unity of the Church only to the extent that in a society of free men a single supreme power of direction with the authority engaging the free conscience of the community represents a principle of unity.

Having said this, we do not mean that the pope can only act when unity is immediately threatened by heresy or schism. This would contradict the teaching of Vatican I that the pope has ordinary and episcopal jurisdiction over the whole Church. Unity is an essential quality of the Church and must be continually exercised at the same time that it is preserved and protected from destruction. All members of the Church contribute to the realization of its unity, not only by avoiding heresy, but by growing in faith and by showing love towards all Christians. This is the bond of unity and peace and the promise of eternal happiness with God.

For the positive, constantly renewed expression of unity

in the Church, the pope has a unique function. He possesses the fullness of authority in the Church; when he puts it at the service of unity, he gives his authority its ultimate meaning, which is the unity found in truth and love. The supreme unifying power of the pope cannot consist in guaranteeing maximum uniformity in administration, rite, scholastic theology, attitudes in spirituality, etc. With his power of jurisdiction the pope must serve the unity which has to be built up in truth and love. That unity is not only compatible with genuine heterogeneity in the Church in the spheres of administration, law, theology, rite, spirituality, etc., but it positively promotes such pluralism. The papacy is neither the source nor the sole channel of all truth and love in the Church, but it can promote growth in truth and love by the means actually available to it, to its organizations and to the man who holds the papal office. The papacy possesses providential gifts and possibilities, including the charisms of the popes themselves. It must hinder developments in doctrine and practice which endanger or destroy unity in truth and love. By its authority the papacy must protect and promote the inner diversity in the Church, because variety is necessary and can be threatened, not only by a false centralizing tendency in the papacy itself, but by many other ecclesiastical trends towards conformity.

Since pastoral theology deals with the whole activity of the Church, and the pope is the highest minister of the office which is indispensable for the pastorale, the question of how papal primacy is exercised is a primary concern for a pastoral theologian. There is no juridical principle which can be legally invoked against the exercise of papal powers before a higher court of appeal. The pope himself determines the extent of his authority, outlines its scope and keeps it within bounds. And yet when the pope is not speaking *ex cathedra,* he may exceed his competence: history shows that papal measures have transgressed universal norms of natural and positive divine law and have been inappropriate in the actual situation. Moreover, we cannot say that an infallible papal definition is necessarily opportune just because it is true. These are indications of how we can search out the non-juridical principles of the exercise of the papal magisterium.

A distinction must first be drawn between the pope's extraordinary teaching office exercised principally in *ex cathedra* pronouncements and his ordinary teaching authority. Since the pope possesses an authentic episcopal authority over the whole Church, he has ordinary teaching authority in regard to the whole Church, and he must exercise it. His doctrinal action cannot be limited to giving the ultimate decision in actual dogmatic disputes; his duty is the positive and active proclamation of the faith to the whole Church in its historical situation. The same thing applies to papal teaching and proclamation of the faith as to papal authority in general: it should not absorb the independent activity of the bishop nor should it assert its position by stifling Christian initiative. The pope in his ordinary magisterium must be careful not to teach in such a way that the doctrine of the bishops and the work of theology is reduced to mere commentary on papal encyclicals and addresses. He should not adopt a detailed position in debates on faith and morals so quickly that in contrast the official and unofficial organs of the development and maturation of faith in the Church — which necessarily work more slowly than the pope's theological advisors — would have to work *too* slowly. Even a doctrinal statement which is not *ex cathedra* represents a real norm for the Church, and so the pope must be careful not to give the impression either that everything is completely open on a question if he has not yet made a pronouncement about it, or else that absolutely no further theological development can take place once he has spoken. If the pope speaks too quickly and too often on particular questions, when he does remain silent it will be interpreted either as bewilderment or as *carte blanche* to accept any convenient opinion. If the pope treats all other teachers in the Church, even the bishops, as his auxiliaries, he is detracting from the divinely instituted teaching authority of the bishops and is paving the way for a monotonous repetition of dogmas and anathemas. In this respect it is interesting to note the differences between the theological elements or characteristics of the teaching offices of the bishops and the pope. The need for plenitude and change, for modernity in the good sense, for a new tone in preaching, for adaptation of the enduring doctrine to the changing historical situation should all be reflected in episcopal teaching. The papal magisterium, on the contrary, has the responsibility of maintaining the *unity* of doctrine expressed in the multiplicity of the religious experience of different theological schools conditioned historically and sociologically.

It is not always easy to distinguish the pope's extraordinary magisterium from his ordinary teaching power because no definite legal form is prescribed for its pronouncements. Moreover, the degree to which a declaration of the ordinary magisterium is binding can be so great that in practice it is almost equivalent to an *ex cathedra* decree. A pope does not define doctrine only to avert a threatening heresy. Although a definition has a limiting character and therefore represents the refusal of a heresy (even if it is made without anathema), this may be but a consequence of the primary intention of a definition, which is to achieve positive significance in an absolute commitment of the Church to a truth revealed by God. An *ex cathedra* document must be a rare measure of the Church's magisterium since a papal definition does not create revelation but presupposes it, guaranteeing explicit certainty and affirmation for those members of the Church who have not yet become fully aware of this particular aspect of the faith. A definition may or may not be timely and it always runs the risk of marking off what is defined from the unity of revelation or of encouraging complacency and smugness.

As a consequence *ex cathedra* definitions will be rare, but especially so at the present time. The religious situation of our time demands (and this applies to the ordinary papal magisterium) a new rethinking and realization of the ultimate foundations and basic truth of the central Christian message. It would be fatal to suppose that no new questions, answers, or reformulations in the contemporary idiom are possible in the ultimate truths of Christianity. Questioning makes it easier for men today to understand what the ancient message of Christianity means to them. In this respect the ordinary magisterium of the pope certainly has duties in domains which previously were recognized as only secondary (e.g., Christian sociology, anthropology, certain marginal sections of moral theology, etc.). These areas are directly concerned with the most urgent decisive questions of Christian belief. In the last 150 years the Church's ordinary magisterium has unfortunately cultivated a soothing traditionalism regarding these problems.

These indications of some of the principles governing the exercise of the papal teaching office are only meant to indicate a regulative framework within which concrete decisions must be made regarding what and how the pope is to teach. In much the same way pastoral theology raises the question of the pope's pastoral office. By pastoral office we do not mean the formal power of jurisdiction, but we are referring to the division of the Church's ministry into the priestly, the teaching and the pastoral offices. The pope's pastoral role is often exercised by the pastoral power of jurisdiction, but is not identical with it since jurisdiction is also exercised in the teaching and priestly offices. Also, the pastoral office is distinct from the teaching office: as teacher the pope gives practical instructions by explicating norms for the Church in action without positing the norms himself; as pastor the pope has authority to give instructions which are binding precisely because it is the pope who gives them. Christian life would be inconceivable without the power of the pope and the Church to establish laws and not merely to announce them.

These norms have to be appropriate and are always open to a generous amount of *epikeia;* they can be dispensed and eventually replaced or even repudiated by contrary laws. The pastoral office is modified essentially by historical, ecclesiastical factors. Regulating the liturgy is quite different from banning a political party. Christians generally presume the pope is within his rights when he speaks and acts. It is a serious mistake, however, in practice to extend the infallibility of the papal magisterium to all doctrinal pronouncements and instructions issued in the exercise of the pastoral office. A tacit encouragement of such an error — e.g., by preventing public criticism — in the long run saps the Church's life, unity and resolve. Today especially in the most important matters it is often impossible to spell out Christian action in detail. More and more often we find ourselves without the pastoral directives which we might wish to have, or else we have to use our own Christian gift of responsibility in interpreting them.

Conflicts are inevitable. Refusing to obey pastoral instructions (at least as regards the letter of the law) is not a denial of the Christian's duty of obedience to the Church's pastoral authority, nor is it a sure sign of incipient heresy or schism. In this domain (as in the whole field of pastoral action) there can be cases where it may not be at all clear which principles apply or which take priority. Pastors, therefore, must be prepared for such conflicts and must handle them with patience. Above all else they should avoid backing the faithful into the false dilemma of either obeying or of refusing obedience *in principle* to the Church's office.

Groping for the truth and wrestling with it are part of the Church's pilgrim existence, part of its pastoral office and part of each individual Christian's search for God. According to Catholic doctrine the authority of the Church, even where its magisterium is infallible, requires the free,

118

believing, conscientious decision of the individual. Doctrine depends for practical efficacy on individual conscience, though it does not depend upon it for doctrinal content and objective authority. It is conscience which accepts the Church's authority as objectively binding, and this acceptance always remains the permanent basis of its efficacy. It should not be surprising, therefore, if a fallible instruction of the Church's pastoral office, despite the obligatory force it possesses *per se,* must be entrusted to the moral evaluation of the individual. *A Christian cannot be absolved from judging whether or not such an instruction is binding here and now.* Of course it is immoral to use this prerogative in order to escape obeying whenever a ruling is not to the individual's liking. But it is also immoral to make an absolute of obedience to the Church's pastors. This distorted theology may have had pedagogical value in more sociologically restricted ages, but it has none today. The Church and its pastoral office are entirely dependent on the good will and the conscience of the individual for their efficacy.

2. The Curia

The pope performs the greater part of his work through Roman institutions ranging from the college of cardinals, the penitentiary, the tribunals and various other curial offices to all the papal commissions. Their work is mainly the concern of Canon Law, but pastoral theology can make a few relevant observations.

Regarding the college of cardinals, the connection between its two functions — electing the pope and serving as his advisory body or senate — is readily explained by history, but this does not mean that it should be taken for granted today. The pope's senate by divine right is the episcopate. Moreover in the contemporary world, which is continually shrinking and yet becoming more complex and difficult to know, those who are best suited to be experts in government of a world-wide Church are those who come from the various areas and know them from personal experience. The bishops of the whole world, or if it is impractical for them to act as an advisory council to the pope, a body representing the universal episcopate is in the best position to help rule the universal Church; such a body does not need to reside permanently in Rome. The college which elects the pope is not, therefore, identical with a papal senate. Conversely, if the pope's senate is thought of as simply the higher officials of the Church's central government in Rome (somewhat analogous to the cabinet of the president of the United States, who alone possesses and retains ultimate authority to make decisions) there is no reason why such a council of ministers should also elect the pope. Historically it is interesting to note that in the first centuries and into the Middle Ages the Roman bishop's function as primate of the entire Church was predominant, while his episcopal function in Rome represented only a secondary office. This ought to be taken into account in the way a pope is elected: the Church as a whole should choose its supreme head, for this is not primarily a matter for the local Roman church.

What is the college of cardinals today — the pope's immediately available advisors or a group holding titular churches because they are functionaries of the diocese of Rome? At the moment the college is still a mixture of men who are selected partly as electoral body and partly as papal officials. Some cardinals combine the two functions and hold curial offices of such importance that they are rightly members of the college of bishops. There are, however, curial cardinals whose work is not important enough for them to be bishops, let alone cardinals, who in fact are the hand-picked group representing the universal episcopate.

Those cardinals who are not mere curial cardinals but genuine territorial bishops together with some curial cardinals who hold high office and are rightly bishops could (if they were sufficiently numerous and were chosen proportionately from the world-wide episcopate) form an electoral body. On practical grounds it is difficult for the universal episcopate to form an immediate electoral body, though it should designate the electors. Today, however, cardinals who are local bishops can be regarded as the pope's advisors only by legal fiction. The curial cardinals, on the other hand, are the pope's highest officials but are not the real representatives of the universal episcopate and are not really competent to represent the whole Church in the election of a pope. Nor is the point at issue the number of Italian curial cardinals. The Church's unity in multiplicity is expressed by the universal episcopate, and this is the fundamental theological principle. It is hoped that Pope Paul's reorganization of the Curia will help to realize this within the Church.

Following the guidelines already established by Paul VI,

pastoral theology can offer several further suggestions. The papal cabinet of ministers and the electoral body could become two separate things, and elections could be carried out by representatives of the universal episcopate nominated by the pope or chosen by the bishops. Or if the college of cardinals is to continue to be both a sort of senate and an electoral body, the appointment of diocesan bishops as cardinals could quietly be dropped and a genuine representation of the whole Church in the papal advisory council of cardinals ensured in other ways. This could be done both by papal nomination and by selections of all the bishops. Perhaps a middle road between these two solutions would also be possible, for it is conceivable that an advisory body to the pope might consist of resident bishops (metropolitans, primates) who would also be the electoral body. These bishops would either be chosen by the universal episcopate or nominated by the pope and would meet from time to time in Rome. In that way the bishops of the Eastern Catholic Churches could share in choosing the pope without being expected to become cardinals, since the office of cardinal does not appear to them to be quite compatible with the dignity of their more ancient position.

What we have said about the college of cardinals has already touched on important pastoral aspects of the other curial institutions. Since from the start there was no intention of describing in detail these institutions (especially the congregations of cardinals) with their different functions and domains, we are not concerned with their canonical structure but with their role and mission in the pastoral action of the Church. The complexities of these departments are striking and difficult to understand, and there is no clear structural principle for these papal agencies. Despite the reforms of the Curia the composition of the Roman government of the Church is still determined by historical factors and still calls for greater adaptation to the needs of the Church at the present time. It is only too easy for the most important tasks of Roman central government to be overlooked or not dealt with quickly and comprehensively enough because there is no clear place for them within the traditional idea of these administrations. In the past curial congregations have had widely diverse commissions extrinsically attached to them without clear demarcation from higher authority. Often these commissions have not possessed a status corresponding to their real importance; often the really important commissions have been difficult to distinguish from less important ones or from those which concern only Rome or Italy. Pope Paul's curial reform should do a great deal to correct the situation.

If curial organizations are really instruments of the pope's universal primacy of jurisdiction over the Church and are not simply Roman or Italian institutions, their composition ought to correspond to the Christian Church which they represent and to the purpose which they serve. For this reason the composition of Roman central authorities should be as international as possible. The ruler of a community chooses his officials from the whole society because he has an equally direct relation to all its members. The internationalization of the Roman Curia will entail difficulties, but certainly the Church of evangelical freedom and love which

123

makes no distinction between nations can carry it out at least as successfully as the United Nations. The greater costs of such an arrangement could be borne by the universal Church, since it is directly interested. Roman central government is very important even today and could well increase in certain respects despite the general need for decentralization of Church administration; nevertheless, only good can come from internationalization of the curial organizations. The Church's universality and genuine pluralism, which are sanctioned in the divine right of the universal episcopate, ought to be exhibited in the composition of the branches of ecclesial power. What we have said has nothing to do with a demand for strict proportional representation. Whether one regards actual representation of the universal episcopate in Rome as desirable or not, the members of a papal administration are officials of the pope and not delegates of the particular churches. This will be true even if these officials are drawn from all countries so as to be in a position to represent the pope's authority over all nations and dioceses effectively, objectively, and in a way that arouses confidence.

A pastoral theologian is well aware that these papal agencies cannot exercise only juridical functions which take the form of laws and administrative decrees. The papacy cannot take the place of free charism in the Church or of the individual character and initiative of the various churches, but it would be a mistake on that account to regard the Roman organizations as mere legislative and administrative instruments, a kind of ecclesiastical civil service. Ecclesial authorities ought to have something charismatic about

124

them because of the nature of the Church, in which even official powers are acknowledged to be gifts of the Holy Spirit. The task of Christian authority is to stimulate, to provide scope for growth, to encourage, to foresee and to attempt to guide future developments even when they cannot yet be the object of laws and administrative measures. Certainly not all new vital tendencies in the Church have come from the papacy, but genuine charismatic impulses have continually flowed from it or have been accepted by it. The same thing should be true of the Curia, and in its internationalization the Curia should have the courage to take in representatives of living forces in the Church, even if they are disturbing and do not readily fit into a bureaucracy.

It might also be suggested that each Roman organization should gather an international circle of advisors. An example can be seen in the consultors to the Biblical Commission, who serve as an international advisory council for the commission's actual members and who keep the commission in genuine contact with actual exegesis throughout the Church. Similar consultative bodies should be organized for other Roman organizations in order to overcome bureaucratic routine. Other papal authorities (e.g., the Congregation for the Doctrine of Faith, the Congregation of Rites, etc.) have consultors from the secular and religious clergy, particularly among the professors of the pontifical universities in Rome, and so are legally international; the mentality is Roman, however, and such a group is no substitute for an international advisory body attached to every curial department.

The papal congregations and commissions have always been conscious of their dignity and authority, which has sometimes led to a certain paternalism, pardonable in the sociological and intellectual milieu of former times but out of place today. The Roman offices must not give the impression that they know everything there is to know, that they are better informed than anyone else or that they do not have to work out practical solutions to difficult problems. They must shed excessive secrecy, as though someone detracts from authority if he has the courage to explain the grounds of a decision. Curial bureaus must also find the fortitude to abandon or radically alter a law instead of maintaining its formal validity by complicated interpretations, amendments and dispensations. They must lose their fear of allowing public discussion of certain problems; a law does not *ipso facto* disappear just because people are allowed to discuss it.

Papal departments ought to be distinguished by those qualities which are taken for granted in any efficient, modern administration: prompt dispatch of business; willing service; scrupulous avoidance of the slightest suggestion of corruption; clarity and simplicity of procedure; avoidance of superfluous ceremonial; a modern system for fixing and defraying costs where these are unavoidable; a sensible handling of the language question in the composition of ecclesiastical documents; permission to use the principle modern languages in letters to Rome; equal treatment for all seeking help. We could also mention the training of personnel in the use of computors and other machines for accurate and efficient research and processing; advice

126

from experts in administration and personnel management of other spreading organizations; training for men in positions of authority that will include a theological as well as a pragmatic and professional orientation. These and similar qualities of a modern administration should also characterize the Roman offices. Internationalization will contribute to making their procedures more equally adapted to different national mentalities than they have been in the past.

In closing, some observations might be made about the relation between the Roman central government and the bishop, as pastoral theology would like to see it. Because the pope exercises full primacy of jurisdiction over the individual dioceses and bishops, the greatest and perhaps most important part of the concrete form of the relationship between pope and bishop is paracanonical in nature. In many domains there are no juridical norms for determining this relation, and in others it is doubtful that there can ever be any. Even where regulations and laws do exist, they are for the most part *ius humanum* by which the pope and his official ministers are not absolutely bound, so that in practice a bishop must always approach Rome at a disadvantage. Much that concerns the ties between Roman government and the bishops is a matter for pastoral theology rather than Canon Law.

The universal episcopate in union with the pope bears the supreme power in the Church and does so by divine right. This prerogative is inalienable and cannot be delegated, any more than the pope's prerogative as head of the episcopal college can be delegated. The universal episcopate as a collegiate body exists only with and under the pope. The Roman bureaus, however, are distinct from the pope and to this extent possess habitual powers in ordinary but human law. They are subordinate officials in relation to the universal episcopate, and although they are not always subordinate to each individual bishop, the general principle has its importance for the relation between individual bishops and Roman authorities. As a member of the episcopal college a bishop has the duty of performing acts of his own which are based on his membership in that college and which affect the life of the universal Church. He must, for example, with the pope be concerned for the missions, for neighboring or particularly needy dioceses. A member of the bishop's college has the duty of going to this college or to its president regarding the affairs of the universal Church. If a bishop submits representations, information, complaints, etc. to the Roman authorities, he is not acting as a subordinate before his superiors. He may be acting precisely as a member of the episcopate to whom the Roman officials are subordinate. In practice, of course, the inter-connections between the rights and duties of a bishop as an individual and as a member of the college of bishops may be impossible to disentangle. The prerogatives of the individual bishop which come from his membership in the episcopal college, must not be overlooked, dis-regarded or pushed into the background by the Roman authorities.

Since the episcopate is of divine right, a principle of subsidiarity holds good for the pope and for his officials, notwithstanding the papal primacy of jurisdiction. This means that the Roman authorities must not take over tasks which the bishop and his diocese can fulfill. Within the range of this principle the demand for maximum demo-cratization of the Church and for maximum independence of the bishops in face of the Roman offices is quite justified. Such a claim does not contest the fact that there are spheres in which Rome rightly reserves all competence to itself, even where it could habitually concede such competence to the bishops, nor does it deny that the final decision about any division of competence lies with the pope. Nevertheless, much of what the Roman authorities reserve to themselves could be left to the bishops in accordance with the principle of subsidiarity. Granted that the global situation of the Church today demands a centralization which was unneces-sary before, the principle of subsidiarity has to be preserved to safeguard the rights of the bishops and to give them some control over the central Roman authorities.

There are two juridically constituted institutions which can form a strong link between the individual bishops and the Roman authorities and can promote both the inde-pendence of the individual bishops and the influence of the Roman authorities on them. It is clear that national bishops' conferences are already a fact of the Church life. In order to function adequately, however, the bishops' conference must be a legal entity with power of jurisdiction; otherwise it is little more than a voluntary assembly whose decisions are merely those of the individual bishops themselves (diocesan law). Bishops' conferences can settle many pastoral and canonical questions and can deal with problems regarding federal government and the social order which exceed the competence and capacity of the single diocese. They can also sponsor missionary and charitable activities in needy dioceses and groups of dioceses. Furthermore, a national bishops' conference protects the independence of the individual bishop and the special character of their dioceses against the Roman tendency to centralization and uniformity. At the same time such a conference preserves at the local level a stimulus from Rome which is necessary today. We hope that Rome will begin to habitually delegate to national bishops' conferences certain powers which at present are legally reserved to itself.

Despite the growing political, economic and cultural unification of the world, continents and cultures are also sharply differentiated. This complexity calls for a corresponding sophistication in the Church's attitude, and bishops' conferences are one reflection of that. The conference's activities can range from advising the Holy See to making absolute decisions requiring no special Roman confirmation. The national episcopal conference is an intermediary authority with close relation to the individual dioceses; if it is not to endanger the independence of the individual bishops and dioceses and in its own way reinforce centralization on a small scale, two things are required. First, the dioceses must be sufficiently large and viable so as not to be compelled to hand over so many rights and duties to the national conference. A diocese could be reduced to the level of a deanery, but this can be avoided by extending or developing the various dioceses. Second, a bishops' conference must possess its own power of jurisdiction so that its decisions are binding on its member bishops. A reasonable system of voting and of reaching decisions will prevent the individual bishop's being out-voted too easily. Once it has been determined which matters fall within the competence of a conference and which do not, then a definite majority can be required as a condition for certain decisions to be binding.

A second legal institution which can bridge the distance between Rome and an individual bishop is the senate representing the universal episcopate and serving as an advisory body for the pope. The members are mostly diocesan bishops representing national or continental bishops' conferences who will assemble in Rome at regular intervals. This senate is concerned with particularly important general questions effecting the whole Church, and so it cannot be too large. Problems of lesser scope should remain the province of the bishops' conferences and the normal papal administration. Too large an advisory body loses its impact and becomes involved in bureaucracy. Membership in the papal senate should be reasonably divided among the territories of the larger bishops' conferences. Vatican II showed that this senate will have to work out the implementation of *change* so that it will be neither too rapid — for thoughtful transaction of business requires time — nor too slow — for new forces and ideas are in demand. As we mentioned before, if the body which elects the pope were suitably organized, this international episcopal senate could coincide with a reorganized college of cardinals. There is no *a priori* objection to the leading officials of the Roman central government belonging to this senate, although the curial authorities should restrict themselves to administrative tasks and leave legislation and ecclesiastical policy to the senate.[4]

In these reflections on the relation of the Roman central authorities to the bishops and dioceses, it is not a question of the legal balancing of the competence of each. The Roman authorities must be willing to accept and to promote a rich variety in the Church's life so that unity in truth and love can characterize the Church in the modern world. The dioceses and bishops have the mission of developing the individual personality of Christian life in a diocese in such a way that the whole people of God is better for it.

Sound thinking precedes live action. In this book we have tried to schematize first a theologically sophisticated understanding of the Church and second an application of this understanding to the Roman Catholic Church as it exists today. In the first chapter we learn that the Church is a community of believers imbued with the Spirit and bound together in hope and love and working their way through history; in the second we consider how this same good news is applicable to the structures and reality of the Church as it has evolved until today.

But none of this is enough. Ideas alone are never the message of the Gospel: Action is. It remains for those who are believers — lay and ecclesiastic alike — to form their conscience and to do their part — each in his own domain — to see the Gospel come to life. As this happens it can truly be observed that the Church grows and develops and there-

[4] Perhaps the universal episcopal senate should be smaller than is desirable for the body which elects the pope; if so, it would be inappropriate to combine the two.

fore lives. Thus will the world, which today as perhaps never before looks to the Church for salvation, recognize in this living community whose actions are inspired by the Gospel a response to its own search for justice and love, forgiveness and tolerance in a world of war and potential conflagration, of prejudice and of poverty, of disease and of unequal distribution of wealth, and of personal loneliness and ennui with life.

Bibliography

CHAPTER ONE

Concilium Series The Church and Mankind, vol. 1.
                        The Pastoral Mission of the Church, vol. 3.
                        The Church and Ecumenism, vol. 4.
                        The Church and the World, vol. 6.
                        Pastoral Reform in Church Government, vol. 8.
                        Spirituality in Church and World, vol. 9.
                        Re-thinking the Church's Mission, vol. 13.
                        Paulist Press, 1965f.

Dulles, A., *Dimensions of the Church,* Newman Press, 1967.

Flanagan, D., (ed), *The Evolving Church,* Alba House, 1966.
Fries, H., *Aspects of the Church,* Newman Press, 1966.

Glock, Ringer, & Bobbie, *To Comfort and To Challenge: A Dilemma of the Contemporary Church,* University of California Press, 1967.

Hamer, J., *The Church is a Communion,* Sheed & Ward, 1964.
Haughey, J., "Church and Kingdom: Ecclesiology in the Light of Eschatology," *Theological Studies* 29 (1968), pp. 72–85.
Houtart, F., *The Eleventh Hour,* Sheed and Ward, 1968.

Küng H., *The Church,* Sheed and Ward, 1968.
Küng, H., *Structures of the Church,* Nelson & Sons, 1964.

Leger, P. E. Cardinal, (ed.), *Theology of Renewal,* Herder and Herder, 1968.

McCarthy, T., *Priesthood of the Laity,* Kenedy, 1967.

McNamara, K., "The Idea of the Church: Modern Developments in Ecclesiology," *Irish Theological Quarterly,* 33 (1966), pp. 99–113.

McNamara, K., "The Mystery of the Church," *Irish Ecclesiastical Record,* 106 (1966), pp. 82–103.

Moeller, C., "History of Lumen Gentium's Structure and Ideas," in *Vatican II: An Inter-Faith Appraisal,* University of Notre Dame Press, 1966.

Rahner, K., *The Christian Commitment: Essays in Pastoral Theology,* Sheed & Ward, 1963.

Rahner, K., *The Christian of the Future,* Herder & Herder, 1966.

Rahner, K., "Christianity and the New Earth," *Theology Digest* (special issue) Feb. 1968, pp. 70–77.

Rahner, K., "The Church a Monarchy?" *Perspectives* 8 (1963), pp. 164–67.

Rahner, K., *The Church after the Council,* Herder and Herder, 1966.

Rahner, K., *The Church and the Sacraments,* Herder and Herder, 1963.

Rahner, K., "The Concept of Mystery in Catholic Theology," *Theological Investigations* IV, Helicon.

Rahner, K., *The Dynamic Element in the Church,* Herder and Herder, 1954.

Rahner, K., "The Lay Apostolate," *Cross Corrents* 7 (1957), pp. 225–47.

Rahner, K., "Sacraments, the Layman and the World," *Theology Digest* 9 (1961) pp. 94–95.

Rahner, K., "Should the Church Solve the World's Problems," *Listening* 2 (1967), pp. 4–17.

Rahner, K., "Theology and the Magisterium after the Council," *Theology Digest* (special issue) Feb. 1968, pp. 4–16.

Rahner, K., *Theology for Renewal: Bishops, Priests, Laity,* Sheed and Ward, 1965.

Rahner, K., "The Unity of Love of God and Love of Neighbor," *Theology Digest* 15 (1967).

Richardson, H. W., *Toward an American Theology,* Harper & Row, 1967.

Ruether, R., *The Church Against Itself,* Herder and Herder, 1967.

Schillebeeckx, E., *Christ the Sacrament of the Encounter with God,* Sheed & Ward, 1963.

Schillebeeckx, E., "A New Type of Layman," *Spiritual life* 14 (1968), pp. 14–24.

Todd, J. M., *The Laity: The People of God,* Paulist Press, 1965.

CHAPTER TWO

Alberigo, G., "The Synod of Bishops and the Structure of Central Government," IDO-C, Doss. 67–7 (Feb. 26, 1967) IDO-C (Information and Documentation on the Conciliar Church) each years offers 20 bulletins on the impact of the Council on Church Structures and 30 dossiers on the impact of the great ideas of the Council on theology. They are available from IDO-C North America P.O. Box 265, Baldwin, N.Y. 11510.

Anon. "Appointment Procedures for Roman Catholic Bishops," *Herder Correspondence* 4 (1967), pp. 113–116.

Berger, P., *Sacred Canopy,* Doubleday, 1967.

Blöchlinger, A., *The Modern Parish Community,* Kenedy, 1965.

Broderick, R., *The Parish Council,* Franciscan Herald Press, 1968.

Brungs, R., *A Priestly People,* Sheed & Ward, 1968.

Canon Law Society, "Towards Constitutional Development in the Church," IDO-C, 68–1, (Jan. 7, 1968).

Chenu, M. D., "Vox Populi, Vox Dei, Public Opinion in the People of God," IDO-C, 67–37 (Dec. 10, 1967).

Congar, Y., *Christians Active in the World,* Herder and Herder, 1968.

Congar, Y., *A Gospel Priesthood,* Herder and Herder, 1967.

Congar, Y., *Power and Poverty in the Church,* Helicon, 1964.

Eagleton, T., *The New Left Church,* Helicon, 1966.

Ernst, C., "Priesthood and Ministry," *New Blackfriars* 49 (1967), pp. 121–132.

Fichter, J. H., *America's Forgotten Priests: What are They Saying,* Harper & Row, 1968.

Greeley, A., *The Hesitant Pilgrim,* Sheed & Ward, 1966.

Greeley, A., *Uncertain Trumpet: The Priest in Modern America,* Sheed & Ward, 1967.

Grootaers, J., "Structures and Living Communities in the Conciliar Church," IDO-C, Doss. 67–15/16 (May 14, 1967).

Hebblethwaite, P., "A Brief Guide to the Reformed Roman Curia," *Month* 39 (1968), pp. 164–171.

Hornef, J., "The Deacon in the Parish, his Relationship to Pastor and Parishioners, *Dominicana* 52 (1967), pp. 254–268.

Hornef, J., "The New Deacon," *Listening* 2 (1967), pp. 137–145.

La Valle, R., "People of God and Politics," IDO-C, Doss. 67–20, (June 18, 1967).

McKenzie, J., *Authority in the Church,* Sheed & Ward, 1966.

Nolan, R., *The Diaconate Now,* Corpus Instrumentorum, 1968.

Nowell, R., *Married Deacons: Does the Church Need them,* Blackwell's, 1968.

O'Donoghue, J., *Elections in the Church,* Helicon, 1967.

O'Gara, J., *The Postconciliar Parish,* Kenedy, 1967.

O'Meara, T., "Karl Rahner on Priest, Deacon, Parish," *Worship* 40 (1966) pp. 103–110.

Pin, E., "The Advantages and Disadvantages of the 'Professionalization of the Priesthood,'" IDO-C, I & II 68–2 & 68–3, (Jan. 14 & 21, 1968).

Rahner, K., *Bishops: Their Status and Function,* Helicon, 1965.

Rahner, K., *The Episcopacy and the Primacy,* Herder and Herder, 1962.

Sloyan, G. (ed), *Secular Priest in the New Church,* Herder and Herder, 1967.

Schillebeeckx, E., *Christ the Sacrament of the Encounter With God,* Sheed & Ward, 1963.

Schillebeeckx, E., "The Synod of Bishops: Crisis of Faith and Local Church," IDO-C, 67–24 (July 23, 1967).

Schillebeeckx, E., "The Synod of Bishops: One Form of Strict but Non-Conciliar Collegiality," IDO-C, Doss. 67–9, (Mar. 12, 1967).

Wakin-Scheuer, *The De-Romanticization of the American Catholic Church,* MacMillan, 1966.

Zizola, G., "The Reformed Roman Curia," IDO-C, 67–8/9, (Sept. 24, 1967).

Index

141